I0570282

LALITAMBA

2019

Lalitamba ISSN 1930-0662 is published annually in the United States by Chintamani Books. The journal is a member of the Community of Literary Magazines and Presses. Issues are printed in accordance with the Sustainable Forestry Initiative. For every magazine purchased, a tree is planted.

Submission Guidelines: Please submit up to five poems or one work of prose per envelope. Include SASE and contact information (name, address, telephone, email). Work should be previously unpublished. We accept first North American serial rights. Kindly post to Submittable or address correspondence to:

Lalitamba
P.O. Box 131
Planetarium Station
New York, NY 10024

Subscriptions are $12 for one year, plus $4.50 postage and handling.

In the Eastern tradition, spiritual seekers don't take personal credit for offering *seva*, or service. A seeker acts as an instrument for the greater good. This is why we don't list staff names on a masthead. The journal is an offering to the immanent and transcendent divine that lives in the heart, and beyond.

Lalitamba is a 501(c)3 nonprofit organization. The journal is donated to prisons and communities in need throughout the United States. *Lalitamba* also partners with Lalitamba Saranam, a holistic women's shelter in New York City. Proceeds from magazine sales are used for these charitable purposes. Further contributions are tax-deductible according to New York State law.

Website: www.lalitamba.com
Facebook: https://www.facebook.com/Lalitamba-252686692751/

The opinions expressed by contributors do not reflect those of the Editor.

Lalitamba 2019
© 2018 Chintamani Books
P.O. Box 131, Planetarium Station
New York, NY 10024
All rights reserved.

ISBN 978-1-7324541-0-1

The name for the journal was inspired by a bhajan sung on a pilgrimage through India.

In early 2004, we traveled through the country with India's "hugging saint" to alleviate the suffering that comes with poverty, illness, and plain loss of hope. The journal was founded when we returned to New York City in November of that year.

The name "Lalitamba" means Divine Mother. In India, the Divine Mother is also praised as jagado dharini, or "She Who Sustains the Universe."

TABLE OF CONTENTS

Essays

LETTERS AND PRAYERS

Aho Mitakuye Oyasin.

All my relations. I honor you in this circle of life with me today. I am grateful for this opportunity to acknowledge you in this prayer.

To the Creator, for the ultimate gift of life, I thank you.

To the mineral nation that has built and maintained my bones and all foundations of life experience, I thank you.

To the plant nation that sustains my organs and body and gives me healing herbs for sickness, I thank you.

To the animal nation that feeds me from your own flesh and offers your loyal companionship in this walk of life, I thank you.

To the human nation that shares my path as a soul upon the sacred wheel of earthly life, I thank you.

To the spirit nation that guides me invisibly through the ups and downs of life and for carrying the torch of light through the ages. I thank you.

To the four winds of change and growth, I thank you.

You are all my relations, my relatives, without whom I would not live. We are in the circle of life together, co-existing, co-dependent, co-creating our destiny. One, not more important than the other.

One nation evolving from the other and yet each dependent upon the one above and the one below. All of us a part of the Great Mystery.

Thank you for this Life.

—Traditional Lakota Prayer

Dear Lalitamba,

The tear drops of innocent children in war bleeds help like no other. Poverty, illnesss, plain loss of hope of children who look for adults to guide them; war, starvation, lust, hate, blood, and bloody water is what they have to cope with. Everybody in this world must stand together. We must fight to overcome, because the future is looking grim. We must stand as one in this stormy weather. Selfish minds are growing strong, but we must fight because good can do no wrong. I hope we can save innocent children, because if you turn to the Middle East and other countries, it should make your soul cry.

Antonio Hatten
Lincoln, NE

Thank God for
fake smiles that
hide real problems

I throw stones
in my glass
house, shattering the

Windows that give
you a view
to all I'm

Sick of. A
Matchstick Man
burned to the

Nub and useless
just trash that
litters the ground

Upon which You
walk

Dan Grote
Waymart, PA

The journal is an offering.
May all beings be joyful and free.

Kristin Camitta Zimet

LOT'S WIFE

Never mind what bargain Abraham
struck with his Father over Sodom.
More than half of us were innocent.

Girl-things to use, dogs chained
or slinking down the alley, never
quick enough, ears back for a blow.

Lot was not the worst. Take your
consolations small, I tried to tell
my daughters. In the marketplace,

hand would squeeze hand, a soft
look light the corner of a veil,
a jar of balm slip from the folds

of a robe into your basket. When
this was your day to be limping,
black and blue, somebody put

her arms around you, pillowing
the hurt without needing a sound.
And so a sweetness underlay

our trouble, an aquifer pooled
under scorching sand. Sustenance,
coolness. Mothering. For them,

my sisters, vaporized, I turned
back to breathe in ash, to bless
the other Sodom that was gone.

Kristin Camitta Zimet

CURRICULUM VITAE

She thought she'd choose the safety of the flat,
skimming the brush across and dipping it
into a scoured jar. The squared canvas,
stretched and stapled with hospital bed corners,
light enough to sling from a single nail,
with all those painted distances pretend.
She knew the comfort of a frame, the effortless
deflections of the glass, fending off fingers.

But then the meaty thickness of her palm
begged to get into the picture, and sketches
were agitating to get out, wiggly lines
scrambling down the bevel, showing off,
and scraps and paper clips and knitting yarn
and spools signed in and bumped against
the backing, so she glued them down
and made a shadow box for them to play in.

But they kept climbing toward her,
over the top of the monkey bars, until
they barged into the studio. Then broken
chairs and lampshades at a tilt wanted
to waltz along, and suddenly her hands
started to swim, scooping up curtains,
splashing the sills and diving into drawers,
popping up toward the ceiling.

They had to saw a seam across the roof,
and flap it open. All of them laddered
out. They took the scaly shingles, plus
the chimney box, the lightning rod,
and the electric poker of the lightning.
Holding hands, they jumped the picket
fences and the hedgerows. The bumpety
hill came lumping up to join them.

Last time I saw her, she and the whole
shebang were dangling by one hand off
a skyhook. She was sculpting purely
out of wind, sloshing up sunstorms,
splattering easterlies, slinging monsoons.
Stars rang a marimba, galaxies joined
the jam, and cosmic rays were showering
confetti. She waved, the lines wide open,
at infinity. Hello, she cried. Come in.

Eve Van Dyke

ART FOR WE

I like to make art with you at night in our bed
when we're cold
and one finds the way to warm the other.
I like to make art with you when I'm alone in my head
after a long day of typing and thinking.
I make art with you when teeth grind
and doors slam
and neighbors hear.
I make art with you when I find that one
little pinch to make us laugh,
or when we make art starting late at night
into the early morning, between sleep.
I make art with you when I'm dreaming,
dreaming of wake and dreaming of sleep
and dreaming dreams
of futures and wide open living.
I like to make art with you when you write
and I listen.
I make art with you when the sun's glare
is too much, and we seek shade,
dripping rides up and down hills,
winding roads into green worlds undiscovered.

Eve Van Dyke

BOOKS AGAIN

I once had a "friend"
who would sneer at me when I
marked a line in my book.
"I would never do that to books," he said.
"They should stay clean, unmarked:
They should remain legible."
I disagree.
Books are meant to be eaten,
and consumed,
and thrown up again.
To be torn and thrown
and lost and borrowed
and found.

Marking books is to scream,
"This is it!"
Marking books reminds you
two years later,
like an old photograph a friend sends
to say, "Wasn't this fun?"

Gregory Gilbert Gumbs

WE ARE NOW MORE AND MORE FLYING
INTO THE GREAT UNKNOWN

We are now all the time more and more flying into the great
unknown, all the time everywhere all the time
like a pilot on a large airplane, which has lost all of its crucial
navigational instruments and constantly
desperately struggles to stay afloat in the angry
warming skies that explode with turbulence

We are now all the time more and more flying into the great
unknown, all the time everywhere all the time
vicariously living amidst the massive ongoing daily fracturing,
the regularly collapsing of the once all-important
sustaining institutions and crucial bridging structures,
that really do make life possible all around us

We are now all the time more and more flying into the great
unknown, all the time everywhere all the time
as the New Economy only booms for that handful
at the very top, who benefit from globalization,
from the low taxes on their exploding incomes and wealth

We are now all the time more and more flying into the great
unknown, all the time everywhere all the time
as the masses left behind in the New Economic Model panic
more deeply every day and then proceed
to flee ever more into dangerously unmoored
political imaginings and longings for a past that never was

We are now all the time more and more flying into the great
unknown, all the time everywhere all the time
as the remaining ordinary resistant people all over are
constantly made fun of on reality TV and talk
shows that show up their cynicism, greedy duplicity,
and utter political irrelevancy

We are now all the time more and more flying into the great
unknown, all the time everywhere all the time
in a still dominant society worldwide, wherein the great
unknown was once invaded and conquered,
wrested from the resisting natives with boundless energy,
optimism, violence, and a profound sense of destiny

We are now all the time more and more flying into the great
unknown, all the time everywhere all the time
while on TV, on the Internet, and in films,
we're bombarded by the rehearsed goings-on
of empty celebrities, untalented stars, and corrupt
politicians willing to sell us anything for a buck

We are now all the time more and more flying into the great
unknown, all the time everywhere all the time
and all we seem willing to do—all of us—is to close the shades,
avert our scary eyes from the clearly expanding chaos
spreading all around us, while we play the latest violent video
games in our cellars

We are now all the time more and more flying into the great
unknown, all the time everywhere all the time
and maybe somewhere out there far in the distance, there might
be some kind of union or joy, or even a sense of justice—but
no, no, nooooo, nowhere around here can any of these things be
detected right now

Gregory Gilbert Gumbs

A SEARCH THROUGH THE U.S.C. LIBRARY SYSTEM

My skin is itching and burning; my thoughts are restless and want
something to eat; the eyes want to see, to think.

—Hannah Villiger

I HAD RECENTLY COMPLETED my M.F.A. in screenwriting at the University of Southern California, and I was awaiting my graduation ceremony, which my parents would attend, flying in from the French St. Martin, the Dutch St. Maarten, in the Caribbean.

One day, in the warm Californian weather, when I had some time to spare on my hands, I decided to finally follow through with a long-held plan, which was to dive into the vast U.S.C. library system and to try and find out if they had any kind of information on my small Caribbean Island of St. Martin, or St. Maarten.

In those days, many Californians liked to visit the small but popular Caribbean island, and I regularly encountered them nearly everywhere in Los Angeles, including at U.S.C. Whenever and wherever I met these Californians, I would tell them that I had grown up in Marigot, the capital on the French side of St. Martin and that I had gone to school in Philipsburg, the capital on the Dutch side of the beautiful little Antillean Island.

These Californians nearly always nodded their heads vigorously and shared one or two telling details with me, to show that they understood what I was talking about. They nearly all told me how much they had enjoyed themselves during their brief time on the "friendly" Caribbean island, as it internationally marketed itself.

In the library, I went to the section that held books about the Caribbean and Latin America. Many of the same books could also be found in the library systems of other leading universities across the United States. Still, on that particular day, I was one of the few U.S.C. students, to be found in this section of the library. I proceeded to look through one book after another for writings about my little French-Dutch Caribbean Island of St. Martin, or St. Maarten.

An old friend, with whom I used to play soccer on the U.S.C. fields in front of the Political Science Department walked by. I had not seen him for some time. He told me that he had completed his Ph.D. in English Literature and was in the process of trying to find himself an academic position at one of the universities in the United States. He passed by, and I continued the search.

I was beginning to despair about ever finding anything having to do with my Caribbean island, so faraway from these sands where I had washed ashore. I sorely missed it. There was quite a lot of information and literature about Cuba, Haiti, Santo Domingo, Jamaica, and Puerto Rico and even about some other islands in the British West Indies, such as Barbados, Trinidad, and Tobago, but everywhere I looked, there was absolutely nothing to be found about the now wealthy and well-developed St. Martin, or St. Maarten.

I felt as if the entire Antillean island on which I had grown up was no more than a mere figment of my exilic imagination.

This gap is often encountered in the history of the maps about the Caribbean region, which reflect the lingering footprints of British colonial history, and often include Caribbean islands much smaller than mine, but never St. Martin, or St. Maarten.

I felt angry and exhausted, and I was just about to throw in the towel, when I saw a book hidden behind some other books at the very end of the shelf. I decided to give my search one last try.

This was a book about travels through the Caribbean during the 1920s by a wealthy white North American couple. They had traveled against the backdrop of the United States' finally becoming the dominant power in the formerly European-dominated geographical area, thus turning the Caribbean Sea into nothing more than a southern version of Lake Superior, or maybe more appropriately, Lake Michigan.

I was shocked, though I should not have been, for I knew the particulars of this vexed evolving colonial and imperial history very well, even before I accidentally happening upon the wealthy white American couple's description of life and of the people, in a sleepy underdeveloped Philipsburg during the mid-to-late 1920s.

I photocopied the passage that this wealthy white American couple had written about St. Martin, or St. Maarten, and I subsequently carried it with me in my shirt pocket for many years. I carried it as an ongoing remembrance of the horror, the horror of this particularly virulently racist imperialist elite white North American tourist encounter in Philipsburg in the 1920s, which in different ways and to different degrees continues to play out today in the form of mass tourism.

Throughout the entire Caribbean region, the popular exotic and packaged notion of "sea, sun, sex, and fun" corrupts and undermines the indigenous cultures of the entire area. An ever more destructive tourist-driven local "hedonistic partying speads and consumes artificial and alienated cultures" in many of the vulnerable Caribbean Islands overwhelmed by mass tourism.

As, I read and re-read the offending passage in the old travel book in the library, I had a hard time believing that I was reading this book in my beloved Los Angeles, which most reminded me of the Caribbean out of all of the places I had ever lived. I continued reading as the couple precisely described the beauty of the magnificent white sand beach of Philipsburg, and especially the undeveloped bay in which they had harbored.

All of a sudden, they switched over to describing the locals who had swum out to their boat, while others approached their large yacht in small fishing boats. They told of the fun they had with them, tossing a few American pennies and other small coins overboard. They described how the "primitive, brutish, and inferior" locals dove into the sea water like uncontrollable wild beasts, viciously fighting with one another for the possession of the different coins, as they couple looked on from up high.

Later on, the American couple invited what they described as nearly naked Dutch Caribbean locals to come aboard their luxurious yacht, to dance and to sing for them, and to entertain them. The wealthy white Americans described the ordinary poor Dutch St. Maarten people as dancing like a set of debased and uncivilized inferiors, braying like wild animals, all the while speaking some form of a barbaric "monkey" English, which they, the highly civilized elite white Americans, could not understand for the life of them.

I was horrified by what I was reading in the U.S.C. library because this virulently racist language was not greatly different from the way in which the Nazis had described the Jews, before proceeding to wipe many of them off of the face of the earth.

I had been educated in the Netherlands, and I knew well the history of Nazism and the Holocaust. I suppose these deeply ingrained racist American attitudes should not have come as any surprise during these Jim Crow years in the United States, when blacks were continually being abused and still regularly lynched.

Still, I had grown up in French St. Martin, where my family was from and still lived, and I had gone to school in Philipsburg on the Dutch side of the Island, where my mother had worked as a teacher. It had never once occurred to me, through my ongoing interaction with many of the elderly folks in Philipsburg, some of whom may have even swum out to the few visiting American boats in the harbor during the 1920s, that anyone of these hardworking, fiercely honest, and wise good people, always free with advice for me, and also deeply proud of the very good work I was doing in the Dutch school, were anything other than good and decent human beings, gifted with all of the strengths and weaknesses that from time to time tend to bedevil each and all of us, any and everywhere in the world

This was for me the very first time in a long while that I thought back on all of these people, many of whom had since passed away. I continued reading this racist imperialist creed about my people, and about my dearly beloved little Antillean island so far away. I was forced to wonder about the ongoing effects that these types of books and writings have on those who happen to read them without my intimate knowledge of the particular people and places in question.

Still, I remained unswayed in my belief of who I was and who my people were. I knew many of these good and decent people well, and I deeply respected them.

I knew that I would fiercely defend them and their fundamental humanity, anywhere and everywhere, and so I began to write.

Ayaz Daryl Nielsen

UNTITLED

evening path into the country
an owl hooting in a maple
apple and cherry trees in bloom
monarch butterflies on milkweed
murmurs from wild geese
grazing on these stilled fields
squat pines in the swamp
hold up a flock of blackbirds
the brown squirrel watches quietly
from the limb a nest rests upon
today's journal entry written full
and sometimes my life opens
its eyes a little bit more

LALITAMBA

Richard Alan Bunch

HOMESTEAD OF SUNS

At the Shearwater Bar and Grille,
we note a fruit basket and sweet
corn that hangs over a bowl's lip.

We order jacket potato, chicken salad,
and Calistoga water.

We hear the swish of sails.
Gulls and other
far-wandering seabirds
cry in the maritime sun
through leaves of the cottonwood.

The beauty of
the floating lotus
that rises out of the mud
like precious pearl
is something we already sense.

Scanning the heavens,
we connect the dots
from the gleam
of unfamiliar years

before numbers became
history's parchment
of radical characters
to exo-planets yet unseen but inferred.

We know outer space
is the homestead of suns
beyond our body's totem of joy
where we may discover
something more spiritual than spirit
and more intelligent than intellect.

This is what happens
when you breathe in
the scent from an ecstatic.

Richard Alan Bunch

RAINBOW TULIP

We note pastured
noontide clouds,
the breaking waves.

From our patio chairs,
tracks of elk
can be seen
on their way
to the roots
of native day,

since the dead
move through
all of us,
including
this dancing sheik,
thoughtful rabbi,
and monkish
flesh of man
beneath a
flowering Judas.

According to
our angel
of suffering creation,
we strain hard

within our
own becoming
to approach
the music
of her grace
in root, rock,
earth and rain.

At the far end
of the sky,
she appears
beyond a field of
rainbow tulip.

Tara Menon

PORTRAIT OF A DEVOTEE

Mornings, afternoons, and evenings,
a lady crosses the street from her home
opposite the *mandiram.*[1]
Her thick, silver-threaded
black tresses reach her ankles
She enters the sanctuary,
her black eyes brimming with devotion to Devi.[2]
Her voice spirals into *bhajans*[3] before the bronze idol
decked in silk, brocade, and jewelry.
The idol's palm upheld radiates blessings to the devout,
to the most earnest one of them all—
the one with the long, silver-threaded black hair,
who returns the gift of her voice
to Devi by singing and singing
with such profound melodic devotion
that others are inspired to pick up the refrain
and match her low, high, slow, rapid,
repetitive, winding, and trailing notes.
Some of the songs are her compositions,
written when her *bhakti*[4] overflowed.
Her voice, amplified by the microphone,
floats through the hall and out of the windows,
mesmerizing passers-by,
uplifting them for a few seconds of their mundane existence.
The pindrop silence at the end of the *bhajan*
is as charged as the music that preceded it.

The lady's life is a rose, plucked petal by petal
and gently tossed at the idol's feet.
Her songs will be sung
even when she is gone,
but who will stoke the devotees' ardor,
fill the walls with hallowed reverberation?

[1]temple
[2]Goddess
[3]religious songs
[4]love for God

Marilyn Ringer

START WITH A TITLE

Think architecturally.
Eliminate words.
Silently say everything

that can be said with gestures,
with scarves swirling, the tilt
of your head, an arched eyebrow,

your eyes, a shrugged shoulder.
Press your hand against your ear.
Listen—the body is singing.

Marilyn Ringer

WHEN I SAY SKY

your eyes ask me to be clouds,
and I become a wisp of thought lost long ago

to uncertain breezes, or to that spirit wind, the one
that lives in red clay caves deep in the *mesas*.

Those tablelands set beneath the dome of heaven
waiting on a god to dine on dirt and light,

the breath of what is human.

I am loosed like branches scrabbled in the wind.
Your breath stirs everything: leaves, limbs, wings.

A storm whirls across the prairie grazing
my hair against my cheek.

Your eyes reflect the clouds.

Jared Pearce

THE BEST WAY TO LEARN IS TO TEACH

The bat flicks the lights so I have to
get up from the couch and chase him
as he goes zipping from room to room.

He leaves his toys on the window
sill, on the furniture, stashed
in the basement, and I'm cleaning

up. He comes, nosing for comfort
out of the cold, then refusing
to lie still, like me.

I get so frustrated that I spank him
on the nose or pinch him until he squeaks,
and then turn him to the stars—

reliable, evenly paced—launching him
up, up where everything
I wish I and he could be is held.

Daniel Patrick Scott

BROWN STUDY

i.

BROTHER GERARD READIES his cell. The cot he carried three flights from the abbey basement is all set up. The small old-style television is moved from its place on the dresser to a corner in the back of the closet and covered up by a comforter he uses on freezing winter nights. The plain wood floor smells of the oil soap he mopped it with. Gerard is surprised by how much he's looking forward to seeing Trevor, who is his first visitor in his seventeen years at Saint Bonaventure's.

Trevor is also his nephew, his sister Angela's oldest, though Gerard has met him only twice before—once as a baby who bawled through his baptism, then again as a boy of ten or so at the funeral of Gerard and Angela's mother. Angela had neatly parted the boy's hair down the middle and used a paper towel to clear his nostrils of dried mucus, leaving them red and tender-looking whenever he poked his head from behind his mother's legs.

"Hello, Trevor," Gerard had said, but the boy only stared back at him with eyes too big for his face. Gerard has no rapport with children. Even when he was that age himself, they were to him contemptuous creatures without decency or pity.

Trevor is twenty-three or twenty-four by now and thinking of becoming a monk, like Gerard. He wants to see Saint Bonaventure's and "find out what a monk does all day." That's the way he put it when he called Gerard out of the blue the day before.

"Will you do me a favor, Uncle?" Trevor added before he hung up.

No one had ever called him "uncle" before, and it moved Gerard in a way he could not have foreseen. "What's that, Trevor?"

"Don't call my mom. She's dead set against my doing this. She thinks I'm visiting a friend in Peterborough."

Gerard had agreed. He probably would not have called Angela, anyway. Their relationship had long since dwindled to a curt exchange of cards at Christmas. Hers, always a picture of the family next to their decorated tree and signed with "Love, Angie" in a way that seemed oblivious to the chasms of time and distance between them. Gerard's card, always the same roughly rendered charcoal outline of the mountains surrounding the monastery, opening up to a blankness that he struggles to fill each day.

He waits. He is slumped in the chair at the small writing desk in his cell, his arms hanging low between his legs. In the desk drawer are the three pages that make up an application to Saint Bonaventure's, the top sheet with the very same outline of the mountains at the top—the design created by a monk who died sometime in the late nineteenth century. Gerard had gone down to the office and had it printed it out from the computer there, in case Trevor turned out to be serious.

The application was the first step to becoming a monk at Saint Bonaventure's, though it was not Gerard's own first step when he had arrived. In his case, that and other formalities had to be delayed for more immediate concerns. The entire bodily deterioration— the trembling, the sallowness, and the hollowed eyes that saw nothing—had to be stopped before anything. There had to be rest and food, which was brought to his cell on brown plastic trays by an unsmiling Brother Vincent.

Gerard had looked into Vincent's eyes and cried for his kindness, but Vincent kept one step away, as if to say, "That's for you to take up with someone far more important than me."

It is a great relief to Gerard not to have to think about that time now, and not ever to have anyone bring it up.

There's a barely perceptible knock at the door followed by a note slipped underneath: "You have a visitor."

Gerard descends the two flights and emerges into the monastery's main lobby. He's taken aback by the sight of his nephew, who is taller, darker, and heavier than the Christmas photos betrayed. He has the same oblong nostrils as Gerard's father did, and the same angular eyebrows that gave his father a perpetually skeptical expression.

They smile and shake hands and Gerard leads his nephew up the stairs to his cell. He finds himself ascending the steps the way he thinks a monk should—calmly, accepting of the physical strain the climb induces.

They reach the landing to Gerard's floor. Trevor is not trying to hide how out of breath he is. "Whew!" he says. "You guys need an elevator—Oh, I'm sorry."

"For what?"

He's whispering now. "I didn't mean to talk!"

"It's alright to talk," Gerard says.

"It is? I wasn't sure if you guys, you know, took a vow of silence or whatever. I mean, the silence is everywhere. I kind of like it. I could get used to it."

"There's no vow of silence, Trevor—although some orders do have that, I suppose. But here at Saint Bonaventure's, the quiet is just the nature of the place."

"Then how come there's these signs everywhere saying 'Silence'?" Trevor had passed the communal dining room on his way in, where there were indeed such signs in large block lettering.

But they're hardly everywhere, Gerard thinks. He is about to say so when he opens the landing door to the long hallway where the monks' cells are. At the far end he sees on the wall a sign requesting silence.

It occurs to Gerard that he has not questioned his surroundings for a very long time. His cell, his mealtimes, his job in the bakery, his prayers—he has not had to think about any of it. That so appealed to him when he first arrived. The people, the routine, the very walls of the place had taken him in with safety and ministration, despite his exhausted, half-starved state, his shame and his self-hatred.

Gerard explains to Trevor that the monastery's guest cells are being used by visitors of the Abbot. "So you'll have to bunk with me," he says.

"Cells?" Trevor says. "Is that what they're called?"

"It's just another word for rooms." Gerard unlocks his door and allows Trevor to enter first.

"Hey, this is kinda nice," Trevor says. The room is no more than a small rectangle of painted wood walls, the bed, the dresser, the writing desk and chair, the closet, and the radiator. On the far wall, a large black-and-gold cross hangs, under which a towel is laid for Gerard's knees, which have been causing him pain for the last couple of years.

The cells were meant to be solemn spaces for prayer and quiet reflection. This had been true in Gerard's case in the early years, and for intermittent stretches thereafter, but in recent years, the intense loneliness of prayer, the physical toll it took on him, and the sneaking suspicion that it didn't really matter had left him shaken.

Then came the day his father had died in his nursing home room, surrounded by all his worldly possessions. Gerard had taken the television set and smuggled it into his cell in a box conspicuously marked "Books." He had been told the monks were not allowed to have television sets in their cells—or radios or computers or telephones. These were considered distractions from service to God.

For the first three months, he was terrified someone somehow knew what he had done, so he kept the television set hidden in the back of his closet. When he dared to take it out and put it on the dresser, he didn't turn it on. When at last he turned it on, he placed a rolled-up towel at the foot of his door to prevent the blue light from giving him away, and he made sure the jack of his father's earbuds was securely inserted to mute the sound. Then, he let it wash over him.

He had watched a lot of television growing up, but now it seemed like a portal to his own private dimension. It filled his senses. It had nothing to do with serving God or prayer or reflection. It was something to occupy himself with at night and to think about during the day.

Now, Trevor approaches the cot. Gingerly he sits on it. It creaks beneath him, and he hops back up.

"That cot won't do for you at all," Gerard says. "I didn't know you'd be so tall. You can have my bed tonight. I'll use the cot."

"Really?" Trevor says. "You'd give up your own bed?"

"Yes, Trevor."

Trevor smiles. "You're not the same as the people out there, Uncle. No one here is. People out there—they're pretty nasty. Do you know what I mean? Do you find people to be like that? It must be so refreshing not to have to deal with that." He heaves his backpack onto the bed. "And people leave you guys alone, don't they? All the way up here in the mountains."

"For the most part," Gerard says.

"I could get used to that, too." He sniffs the air. "It smells like bread in here," he says.

Gerard doesn't smell a thing. Although he works every day in the Saint Bonaventure's kitchen helping to bake the bread that the monks sell to area grocers—Bonnie Bread, they call it—he hadn't known that he carried the smell with him to his cell.

Gerard takes a seat at the writing desk. "Why do you want to become a monk, Trevor?"

Trevor sits on the bed. "I'm not sure I do," he says. "But sometimes, especially lately, I have this feeling of wanting to do the right thing, and wanting to be around other people who want to do the right thing. People like you."

"And what about God?" says Gerard.

"Well, God is a given, right?"

"The life of a monk is a life of service to God. It's not just a way to get away from it all. There are deprivations you'd have to get used to."

"You mean like no computer, no phone? I mean, other than the one in the lobby."

"And no television and no radio. And no girls. Do you think you can live a life of celibacy, Trevor?"

"Absolutely, Uncle." That's the most convincing thing he's said, Gerard thinks.

"Sex and television and cell phones—they only lead you away from God, right?" Trevor continues. "I mean, they're just distractions from what's really important. They're small, momentary pleasures that leave you empty and disappointed in the end, right?"

For a moment, Gerard thinks Trevor sounds like the Abbot, or like Father Decatur, the parish priest he had served as an altar boy growing up in East Boston. Suddenly it is not hard to see Trevor in the role of monk.

A bell rings. It seems to come from nowhere and everywhere. Trevor looks around.

"That's supper," Gerard says. "You must be hungry."

Trevor breaks into a smile.

At supper, Trevor is almost aggressive in his determination to remain silent. He taps one monk on the arm, gesturing at the butter with mime-like exaggeration. To Gerard's surprise, the brother is not annoyed at having his meal interrupted but actually smiles gently at Trevor. Trevor smiles back. In fact, no one seems to mind his presence there, despite how much he is eating, or that his elbows are on the table.

Gerard had no such appetite on his own first day at Saint Bonaventure's. The half-spoonfuls of watery broth administered to him by Brother Vincent were all he could manage. The fussy way Vincent dabbed his chin with a napkin reminded him of his mother. He said things like "that's good" and "come on now"— not especially kind words, though not meant to be unkind either. Not like those spoken by the people from whose presence he had just been removed.

Later that night, Gerard is kept awake by Trevor's asthmatic breathing. The cot is more uncomfortable than he'd imagined. It is so low to the floor that he can't see Trevor up on the bed.

He mulls over the possibility of Trevor's coming to Saint Bonaventure's. He has arranged a meeting for Trevor and himself the next day with the Abbot, even though Gerard hates talking to the Abbot. Their conversations always seems to come to a point where Gerard feels it would have been better if he hadn't said anything.

Sleep does not come. The cot creaks and wobbles as Gerard turns onto his side. He wonders what's happened on the television show he usually watches in the early evening.

ii.

IN THE MORNING, as his nephew sleeps, Gerard rises and showers in the communal bathroom down the hall. What seemed yesterday to be possible—perhaps even likely—looks ridiculous today: Trevor is not serious about joining the order. He probably just needs some time to himself, or maybe a break from his mother. In fact, Gerard feels foolish at having believed. He knows that this has been a problem for him in the past, believing too easily the things people tell him.

When he returns from the shower, Trevor is awake and dressed, sitting on the edge of the bed and looking down at a cell phone.

Gerard laughs gently. "There's no reception up here, Trevor," he says.

"Sure there is. I just got off the phone." He stands up and slips it into his jeans pocket.

"Oh. You called your mother?"

"No. Just texting someone. A friend."

Gerard dresses in his black habit, fastening the belt around his waist, followed by his black scapular.

Trevor looks at him as if noticing his clothes for the first time. "So that robe," he says, "—doesn't that get hot?"

"Sometimes."

"And the monks have to wear them all the time?"

"Pretty much."

"Even when you're working at the bakery?"

"Well, I take off the scapular and put on an apron."

He takes up a small Bible from his desk. He likes the feel of its soft leather cover. He lifts the rosary hanging from a peg in the wall.

"Is that where you're going now?" Trevor says.

"No. It's time for lauds."

"For what?

"Morning prayers. After that, breakfast. Then, I go to the bakery."

"Can I come with you to—what is it?—lauds? I mean, wouldn't that be a good thing for me to experience?"

As they walk to the monastery chapel, Gerard again finds himself feeling self-conscious about how he is moving. Does he look pious enough? How sinful is it to be worried about such a thing?

The chapel is easily the most impressive thing about Saint Bonaventure's. The golden walls reach to octagonal stained glass windows that slant upward to a pinnacle. Suspended from the center is a giant gold cross, hung as if it were floating in the air, though the wires that hold it in place are visible.

There are a few other monks in the pews. Most prefer evening prayers, but not Gerard: They conflict with the television show he's been watching.

Gerard and Trevor take a pew and kneel in silence. Gerard immediately closes his eyes, hoping to induce an honest reverie like the ones that used to grip him, but he can only think that this is another performance he is putting on for Trevor. Is this how it would be if Trevor actually did come to Saint Bonaventure's, to stay?

He remembers the first time the reverie happened. He had been at the monastery just over six months. He was measurably recovered, but almost all of that was physical. Spiritually, he was still in a delicate condition. He was beginning to wonder if he were seeking God or simply solace.

Lying on his bed in his cell one night, he sat up suddenly. He felt the presence of God so keenly that he swooned and slipped off the bed. His body twitched as he felt the ecstasy coursing throughout his body. It both tickled and stroked him lovingly, and he lay splayed across the floor.

For hours, he would lie there barely able to move. He would whisper things like "Okay" and "I understand" and "I love you so much." Sometimes he drooled on himself.

As the reveries continued, nightly for weeks and even months, he learned to crawl to the cross on his wall and pull himself up enough to kneel in prayer. During the daytime, he kneaded dough and went about his other business in a rarefied realm, which no one asked him about. He was grateful that they took no particular interest.

But nothing like that has happened to Gerard in a long time.

In the pew there with Trevor, Gerard begins to play scenes in his head from the television show that so involves him lately. He keeps his eyes closed.

He hears not a sound next to him. He begins to suspect that Trevor has risen and left, but when finally Gerard opens his eyes, Trevor is still there, kneeling. His head is bent toward the floor, clasped fists pressed to his forehead, tears streaming from his tightly shut eyes.

At breakfast, it occurs to Gerard that Trevor has adjusted well to the silence. He wears an expression on his face that says he has much to say, but no intention of speaking. They do not speak again until after breakfast, when they are back in the cell.

Gerard finds a note that has been slipped under the door. He sits at his desk as he reads it.

"It looks like the Abbot has to reschedule our meeting," he says with some relief. "He's too busy with his own guests today. He's hoping to do meet tomorrow, instead."

"Is that a problem for you, Uncle?"

"No. You can stay here as long as you like, Trevor."

"Thanks. I'll take the cot tonight."

"You'll never fit into it," Gerard says. "It's alright. I don't mind the cot. You can come to the bakery with me if you like."

"I think I'll stay here. Maybe wander around the place a little, if that's alright."

"Suit yourself."

"If I become a monk, will I be baking bread, too?"

"It depends what you're assigned to. You'll do whatever needs to be done."

Trevor nods.

While at the bakery, Gerard is surprised to find he is in a state similar to the reveries of old—dreamy, self-contained, oblivious to the others who go about their business all around him. Nobody notices the slight smile on his face.

At the end of the workday, Gerard returns to his cell. He has an hour until suppertime. He stops at his door to fish the key from his wallet. He doesn't have a keyring, and he doesn't need one. His cell key is the only key he carries.

He halts when he hears voices on the other side of the door. At first he thinks Trevor is talking on his cell phone, but then he notices the blue light of the television shifting beneath his door. Panicking, he struggles to open and close the door quickly yet quietly.

Trevor is lying on the bed with his arms up behind his head, his eyes glued to the small television set Gerard keeps hidden in his closet. The television set is now sitting on his writing desk. Trevor is watching a Red Sox game.

"Trevor! What are you doing?" Gerard dashes toward the flickering screen and snaps it off.

"Take it easy, Uncle. I just got bored and decided to watch some TV."

"But that"—he gestures at the small black box—"was in there"—he points to the closet.

"Yeah. I happened to notice it in there. I didn't think you'd mind."

"But..." Words fail him. He sits on the bed. He feels a little sick.

"Hey, don't worry, Uncle. It's not a big deal."

"I just...I'm not supposed..."

"...to watch television, I know. But so what? You broke one little rule. You think you're the only one? I bet you're not. And who are you hurting?"

"It's an insult to God."

"You really think God cares if you watch TV?"

"Please keep your voice down. What I'm saying is, I took a vow to serve God fully and without condition. I vowed to stay near to Him always. When I watch TV, I forget myself and I forget Him." He blinks his eyes several times to hold back his tears. "And still, I can't stop."

Trevor puts his hand on Gerard's shoulder. "I'm not gonna tell anyone that you have a TV in here," he says.

It is easy, Gerard finds, to believe the things that come out of Trevor's mouth. They are spoken with a self-assured tone that again reminds Gerard of Father Decatur.

Trevor says, "Anyway, I'll put the television set back in the closet."

"No," Gerard says. "It's okay." Gerard gets up and goes to other end of the cell, where the cross hangs. He takes the rolled-up towel from the floor and lays it in front of the door, blocking the space beneath the door. Trevor leans forward and snaps the television set back on.

They sit in silence as they watch. Gerard knows next to nothing about baseball, except that everyone he grew up around was mad about it, but the images dance in his eyes and the sounds tickle his ears, even when kept low. More than that, he's sharing them someone, pure and unashamed. For a long time, television was a secret that he harbored with a special intensity.

At supper, Trevor exhibits the same silent knowing as he had that morning.

Gerard falls asleep easily in the cot that night, thinking that he will wholeheartedly recommend his nephew to the Abbot.

iii.

BUT FOR THE NEXT couple of days, the Abbot's time continues to be monopolized by his guests. Appointments are made and then broken. The Abbot is like that: remote, hard to track down, like God himself.

In his first days at the monastery, Gerard lived in terror waiting for the Abbot to come to him in his cell as he had been told the

Abbot would eventually do. After perhaps two weeks, the Abbot knocked on Gerard's cell door and then opened it without waiting for a response. Gerard was sitting on the floor next to the bed, his back against a wall, his knees drawn up to his chest. His eyes were cast down onto the floor. The bed was sheetless. Its linens sat folded on the mattress, still in the condition Brother Vincent had brought them several days before.

The Abbot looked down at him. Gerard could not get himself to look back.

"I've spoken with Father Decatur," the Abbot said, "about your situation at the university in Pennsylvania. What was your course of study there?"

When Gerard only winced, the Abbot said, "Answer me!"

"I...um...theology."

"So you wished to be a theologian?"

"A teacher, sir."

"But then, you thought differently."

"Yes, sir."

"And what was it that caused you to change your mind?"

Gerard's eyes glassed over with moisture. "I was so hungry..." he said. "My head hurt so bad... And I bruised my arm. It only got worse. It never got better."

He gripped his arm and glanced up at the Abbot, whose expression had not changed at all.

"And they hated me for it," Gerard went on. "In the dorm, in the classrooms. The students, the professors—they hated me for things I had no control over. And I...I stank, Reverend Father, sir. I didn't know what to do. I tried to get rid of it. I didn't know where it was coming from. I can smell it right now. I know you can, too."

"Don't presume to tell me what I can or cannot do. If you were hungry, why didn't you eat?" the Abbot said.

"I had no money."

"How did you pay to go to the university, then?"

"Father Decatur got me a scholarship of some kind, but it didn't pay for my food. My father was supposed to do that. He was supposed to send me money. I waited. None ever arrived."

"Why didn't you call and tell him?"

"I'm not sure. I just knew he'd get angry hearing from me."

Gerard's father had never wanted to him to go to college. He himself had received no education past the seventh grade, and he wanted Gerard to get a job and contribute money to the household. But Father Decatur had told Gerard's father that his son was a bright prospect who deserved to be nurtured.

Father Decatur no longer seemed to hold this belief as they drove the long road from East Boston to the monastery in the White Mountains of northern New Hampshire. Gerard sat gaunt and shivering in the passenger seat. The former star altar boy felt no forgiveness from his mentor, just the sadness at his having been so wrong. "Being a good priest is about reading and understanding people," Father Decatur had once said to him. He was probably thinking now of how badly he'd misread Gerard.

The Abbot said, "Do you believe you could live a life completely and unequivocally in the service of God?"

"Yes," and as Gerard answered a smile contorted his face, and he almost wanted to laugh. "Please yes, please. There's nothing I ever wanted more."

"And does this desire supersede all other desires for you?"

Gerard nodded over and over as the tears streaked his face.

The Abbot turned to go. "You will be given further instructions."

"But...can I stay? Father Decatur said—"

"Father Decatur does not make the decisions here. As I said, you will be given further instructions. Get up off the floor, and put those sheets on the bed. What do you think they're there for?" The Abbot's tone softened somewhat. "The showers are down the hall," he said, then shut the door behind him.

Gerard prays now that the Abbot be kinder to Trevor than he was to him.

In the stretch of days that follow, it seems to Gerard that Trevor has grown quieter and less inquisitive about monastery life. Gerard prays and works in the bakery as usual, then returns to his cell to find Trevor watching television, pecking away at his cell phone, or sleeping.

At one point, Trevor does not appear to be in the room at all until Gerard switches on the light and finds him crumpled on the floor in the far corner, near the hanging cross.

"Trevor, what are you doing?" he starts.

But Trevor does not answer. Instead he peers at his uncle.

"Trev—"

"I'm just thinking, alright?"

"Alright." It is the first time Trevor has ever expressed anything like impatience toward Gerard.

Gerard is hurt, but he understands: Trevor isn't sure if he's doing the right thing. He doesn't know if he's up to it. It would be a big decision for anyone, whether to become a monk or not, though for Gerard it had not been a decision at all.

Or Trevor is overwhelmed by reverie. He is on the floor because this is the fastest, readiest freedom from gravity, the last force between himself and God.

Gerard would probably have responded the same the way had anyone tried to disturb him in such a state.

After supper, they do not talk much. They watch television until it is time to go to sleep. In the middle of the night, Gerard wakes to the light from Trevor's phone coloring the ceiling. There is no rule against guests using such devices, Gerard thinks, including, for that matter, the television.

iv.

GERARD'S ONE DAY OFF during the week is sunny and brisk. Trevor, for the first time, declines to go to prayers, saying he needs to sleep. Sensing his nephew wants some time alone, Gerard decides to attend a daylong retreat with several other monks in a nearby wooded area. These are affairs of outdoor prayer and grilling on the small Hibachi owned by the monastery. They take place every Saturday, when the weather allows, though Gerard has never partaken, until now. He is surprised to find himself enjoying the gathering. Then, the Abbot, whom he had not noticed was there, approaches him.

"Brother Gerard," the Abbot says. "What a surprise. Is your nephew beginning to cramp your style?"

"What? No, Reverend Father. I mean..." His voice trails off. He is unsure of what the Abbot is asking him.

"My guests are leaving today," the Abbot says. "You can bring—what's his name? Trevor?—by my office tomorrow at two."

"I'll be at the bakery at that time."

"Just tell him to be there. Your presence isn't needed."

"Yes, Reverend Father."

"Where is he now? At the chapel? I've heard he's been spending his days there, while you're at the bakery. I've seen him there myself."

Gerard didn't know that. Trevor was always in the cell watching television when he came in in the evening.

"He's a lot like you, isn't he?" the Abbot says.

"I don't know what you mean, Reverend Father."

"An unstable sort. I've heard several reports of his being in tears at the chapel. Once he even had to be helped back to your cell by Brothers Norman and Andrew."

"I'm sorry, Reverend Father. I had no idea."

"I'm not running a home for the mentally addled here, Brother Gerard."

"Yes, Reverend Father. I think he was just...moved by the spirit."

"Oversensitive types, in my experience, make for poor monks. Monastic life should be one of wholly accepted joy, don't you agree?"

"Oh yes, Reverend Father."

"We also frown on accepting relatives of the brothers. Still, I won't know for sure until I meet and talk with him. Tell him not to be late."

Gerald nods.

"Do you want him here, Brother Gerard?"

"Me? Oh well, I...I don't think..." And just as always, his attempt at talking with the Abbot crumbles to nothingness. "Whatever you decide will be fine with me, Reverend Father."

The Abbot rolls his eyes slightly as he walks away.

When Gerard returns to his cell in the late afternoon, Trevor is slipping his cell phone into his pocket.

Gerard smiles weakly. He feels it best not to pry. If Trevor is coming to the conclusion that this life is not for him, he should reach that point on his own.

Trevor makes an effort to smile back. He says, "So what do people do around here when they're not..."

"...serving God?"

"Yeah."

"I imagine the brothers all have their private pursuits," Gerard says.

"Like what? I mean, do you ever—I don't know—go anywhere? Are you allowed to have a car?"

"The monastery has a van that we use to deliver the bread every Friday. The brothers can also sign out to use it if they need something from town."

"Do you ever do that?"

"Me? No, no."

"Why not?"

"I don't know how to operate a car, for starters. I don't have a driver's license."

"Why not?"

"I just never got around to it, I suppose."

"So what do you do if you need something from town?"

"One of the other brothers will drive me. One of the brothers who has a driver's license, of course."

"What about a guest of one of the brothers? Could I sign out the van if I wanted?"

"Yes, but I would have to go with you if you did that."

Trevor seems to consider this for a moment. Then, he hops down from the bed and says, "Well, let's go then!"

"No, Trevor."

"Why not? Today's your day off, and I'd like to see what the town's like. All I saw was the bus station when I came in."

"I don't know."

"Look." Trevor digs out his wallet. "Here's my driver's license, so you know I'm legal. Come on, Uncle. God has given us this beautiful day." He flashes a smile, just as he had upon first arriving at the monastery.

Gerard can't come up with a good reason not to, besides his own natural hesitation. He notices that Trevor has brought up God again, which he also hasn't done since first arriving.

"I do need a few things from the drugstore," he says. Perhaps a drive would help restore Trevor's good will, and if Trevor wanted to, they could discuss his upcoming meeting with the Abbot.

"Great," Trevor says. "Don't you want to change first?"

Gerard looks down at his habit. For the first time, he senses disgust toward the cloth on Trevor's part. There is no rule forbidding the monks from changing into civilian clothes when they go into town, but Gerard feels more comfortable in his robe, and he's noticed that the people at the drugstore treat him more kindly when he wears it.

The van is a twenty-year-old model with "St. Bonaventure's" stenciled on the door of the driver's side. It has not a dent or ding, but shows its age in the ripped seats of its interior. The back of the van is stacked with metal trays that are used to carry the bread. Even empty, the van smells faintly of freshly baked loaves. Trevor wrinkles his nose and lowers both the driver's side and passenger windows.

Once they are on the road, the wind from the open windows begins to whip violently through the van. Trevor seems to revel in the sensation. His red hair looks like a fire that is desperately trying to escape consuming itself. Gerard's habit slaps and billows. He thinks Trevor is driving too fast, and he says so.

Trevor pauses for a moment before saying, "I'm just doing the limit, Uncle."

"It seems faster than normal."

"How would you know what normal is?" Trevor says. "You don't even know how to drive." There is a tartness to his words that Gerard has not heard before. "I've been driving since I was fifteen," Trevor goes on. "But of course you wouldn't know that. I mean, it's not like you were ever around when I was growing up."

Gerard is speechless. Trevor, having had enough of the maelstrom, presses the button that rolls the windows up until they remain only slightly open, with air blowing through small strips at the top.

"I'm sorry for that, Trevor," Gerard says. "I should have made more of an effort to stay in touch with you and your mother."

"No worries," he says, seeming to regret his tone. "I know things have been tough for you."

"Why do you say that?"

"I don't know. That's what my mother always says about you."

"Oh. I wonder why she would she say that?"

"I don't know. But come to think of it, my mother says a lot of stupid things."

Gerard smiles. He's glad it is Trevor who says this and not him. He's never liked Angela, precisely for the things that come out of her mouth. She has a nasty predilection for ridicule.

Gerard stares out the window in silence. He is not sure how much time has lapsed, when they pass a strange local monument, a badly smashed pickup truck erected on a granite pedestal that raises it high enough to be seen by the cars passing on the highway.

On the front of the pedestal is a white cross and a sign with the hand-painted words "Please Don't Drink and Drive." The scene is a rendering of unsurvivable violence that made a strong impression on Gerard the first time he saw it—on the drive from East Boston years ago with Father Decatur. At the time, Gerard had found it impossible not to imagine the terrible truths that had transpired in those twisted folds of metal. This was the first time since the university debacle that Gerard had been able to draw out of himself, even if only briefly, to feel someone's misery besides his own.

But the monument, Gerard suddenly realizes, is quite far past the exit to town. He pops up in his seat. "You missed it," he says. "You missed the exit, Trevor."

"I didn't miss it. I only passed it."

"But that exit is the way to town."

"I know, but it's such a nice day I thought we'd just go for a drive."

"To where?"

"I don't know. Nowhere in particular. Haven't you ever just gotten into the car and gone for a drive before?"

Of course he hasn't. Trevor knows that.

"Trevor, please turn around." Gerard knows he has a tendency toward carsickness if he rides for too long.

"Why? Can't you just sit back and enjoy the ride for once?" He presses a button on his door that rolls the windows back down. The wind buffets Gerard's face. The world is racing by, missing him only by inches.

"Trevor—please slow down."

"I'm doing the limit," Trevor says, but he is not.

Gerard can see clearly that he is doing seventy-five—twenty miles over the speed limit. The metal trays are rattling in the back.

"Everything's fine, Uncle. Don't worry so much."

"Trevor, I want to go back to the monastery."

"I can't do that, Uncle. Not yet." Trevor's voice takes a turn, dropping a register and lapsing into what Gerard recognizes as that East Boston bluntness he grew up around.

"Trevor—"

"Now listen up. I'm not turning this van around, and I'm not going any slower than I am right now. That's the way it is. So sit there, and stop talking."

Gerard hears the contempt rumbling beneath Trevor's words. Not since the university has such disdain been directed toward him.

The car speeds on, tires whining over the asphalt. As the wind slaps at him, Gerard sinks into his seat. A mortification falls over him that precludes speech.

This stasis stays with him even through Trevor's stop at a gas station. "You want a coffee or something?" Trevor says. "You need to go to the bathroom?"

But Gerard can only sit, slumped, unable to look Trevor in the face.

v.

IT'S NOT CLEAR TO GERARD how much time passes before he is able to see again what is plainly in front of him: the glove compartment, the dashboard, the New Hampshire state inspection sticker adhered to the filthy windshield. When he looks up, he sees the approaching city of Boston. Unfamiliar skyscrapers crowd together. This is not the Boston he grew up in, nor even the Boston of his last visit, more than a decade ago, to attend his mother's funeral.

Trevor expertly maneuvers his way off the interstate, driving as if he knows exactly where he is going. On the city streets, he must and does drive more slowly. Gerard, clears his throat and asks, "What are we doing here, Trevor?"

"I have to see someone" is Trevor's terse answer.

The slowing speed eases Gerard's mind somewhat. He looks over at Trevor. "I guess you're leaning toward not becoming a monk now," he says.

"I wouldn't say that."

"You haven't shown much interest in preparing for your meeting with the Abbot."

"What's to prepare? He'll either like me, or he won't. If he doesn't, it's not the end of the world."

"Trevor, I really think you don't have any idea as to how these things work."

"Do you? You entered the monastery after you cracked up. How prepared were you when you met the Abbot?"

Gerard sinks away, shamed. He has been a fool to think Angela wouldn't have told Trevor everything—or at least as much as she knows. He should have learned by now that people can't help but talk.

Trevor abruptly turns into the parking lot of an apartment building. He backs the van into a space. Most of the other cars are parked the same way, as if a quick getaway were essential. "I won't be long," he says and gets out, leaving the keys in the ignition.

He glances from side to side, then jogs to the building's front entrance. The double doors are two large sheets of shining glass.

Gerard leans forward and gazes up the length of the apartment building, which rises five or six stories. He has never had to rent an apartment before. He can't help but wonder what the apartments are like, if they are one or two rooms or more, if they are clean or messy, if they are drafty in the winter.

Some of the windows have curtains or blinds drawn over them; other frames reveal reflective panes. Air conditioners jut out sporadically.

He becomes faintly aware of a person in the car parked next to him. He turns and sees a young woman. Her head is cocked against the steering wheel, and she appears to be unconscious. In the seat behind her, a toddler is strapped into a car seat, awake and apparently content.

At first Gerard is struck by the woman's deadness, but then he senses movement underneath her eyelids. She may be just sleeping. She is young, and the baby is secured as if by a good mother. She may have reached her limit, stopped and taken a respite from her exhaustion, even if just for a few minutes.

A yellow car pulls into the parking lot and circles the building. The driver seems to be looking for a place to park but passes by several open spaces. Then, the car heads out into the street again and drives off.

Gerard hears a high-pitched but muffled ringing. He opens the glove compartment to find a cell phone. It looks nothing like Trevor's, which appears to be a blank screen—this one must be an older model. Buttons that flash wildly as it rings.

Gerard remembers now that the van should have been returned hours ago. He holds the cell phone in his hand, unsure of which button to press to answer the call. He pushes at them frantically, but the phone goes silent and dark. He puts it back into the glove compartment.

He looks up to see Trevor coming out of the apartment building. He is walking quickly with his head down. Once he gets into the car, Gerard sees that he has tears in his eyes.

"Trevor, what's the matter?"

Trevor shakes his head. "Nothing," he says.

"It doesn't look like nothing."

"Believe me, you wouldn't understand."

"I think I might."

"How can you? You've never been in love. You don't know what it's like. You don't know what anything's like. You can't even drive yourself to the goddam drugstore. You can't even watch television without being afraid you'll go to hell for it. You're messed up."

Suddenly Trevor jumps out of the car, slams the door, and runs out of the parking lot.

"Trevor!" Gerard scrambles out of the car. "Trevor! Where are you going?"

Trevor keeps running. Gerard hears his sobs growing fainter, until they dissolve in the air.

Gerard looks about. He wraps his habit around him—it's starting to get chilly as night falls. He walks to the entrance of the parking lot. Trevor is nowhere in sight. He looks up and down the street, his eyes stopping at a lighted sign that reads "Billy's Gas."

The name is unfamiliar to him, but the sign itself—the shape of an inverted bowtie—and the pole itself, which narrows as it rises, strike him as familiar. He remembers watching the forlorn face of Father Decatur as he pulled up to the pumps and filled his car before their drive to the monastery. And he sees it now—the church that stands on the next block down, its spire piercing the darkening sky over the one-and-two-story buildings that surrounded it. St. Michael's, his boyhood parish.

He half-expects to see Father Decatur descending the steps, but Gerard knows he had long ago been transferred to a parish in Maryland.

He is in East Boston, of course. He is in the neighborhood he grew up in. He knows that his parents' house—or whoever's house it is now—is three blocks left after the gas station. He turns to look up at the apartment building and realizes it was not here the last time he was. It has been built of new brick and stands out from the windowless clapboard houses around it.

Angela did not move far from their parents when she got married. He knows the address—159 Bennington Street —because of the years of Christmas cards they have exchanged. He heads off in what he believes is the right direction. The air is cool and dark when he reaches Angela's house, which looks exactly as he remembers it, although he has only been there a few times over the years.

He hesitates but knows he has nowhere else to go, so he walks up to the door and reaches for the doorbell. It sounds loudly enough to wake up the entire street.

Angela opens the door

"Hi, Angie."

"Hi, Jerry. Trevor told me he went to stay with you. Well, come on in. We're not heating the great outdoors here."

She sounds just the way their mother used to. Gerard follows her into a warm room with a television and two easy chairs parked in front of it. The living quarters are tighter than he remembers. She takes a chair and tells Gerard to take the other one.

"Where is Trevor?" he says. "Is he okay?"

"He's in his room. He's broken up, but that's life. Is that what they make you wear at the monastery?"

"I'm afraid so. What is he broken up about?

"A girl. Pam's her name."

"She broke up with him?"

"I hope she did, but who knows? They tend to go back and forth a lot, those two. Basically she's got him wrapped around her finger. So, Trevor's been up there with you all this time?"

"He told me he was thinking about becoming a monk."

Angela snorts. "Yeah, he's been on some kind of religious kick ever since Pam told him she was pregnant. I told him no amount of polishing the pews at St. Michael's is going to change anything."

"So, Trevor's the father."

"That's what she says. Personally, I wouldn't put it past her to lie about it—she's a very unsavory person, Jerry. She lives in that new apartment building on Belmore. Been a lot of drug activity there. It's been on the news. But Trevor said he was sure the child was his. He cried that he wasn't ready to be a father. I told him, ready or not, here it comes. Trevor didn't tell you any of this?"

"No."

She shakes her head. "He was running from his problems, like he always does. He said he needed to go away for awhile and think. I said the time for thinking is passed, Trevor. He didn't even tell Pam where he was going. She came here demanding to know where he was. Even if I had known, I wouldn't have told her. She's not coming into my house demanding anything. So before she left, she called me a bitch—this is the mouth on her—and told me if Trevor ever came back I could tell him she had an abortion. She said it just like that, Jerry. Like it was nothing. The woman is wicked. Then she slammed my front door so hard it I thought it would come off its hinges. Thankfully, she hasn't been back since."

Gerard sits back. He remembers Trevor's preoccupation with his phone. He remembers the way he carried it in his pocket everywhere he went, even to morning prayers.

"And," Angela continues, "apparently, she went ahead and did it. Had the abortion. That's what Trevor told me, tonight."

That explained the tears.

"You're not going to drive all the way back to New Hampshire at this hour, are you? Why don't you stay a day or two. You can sleep on the couch. I can get you a pillow."

The smile he manages is genuine. She has forgotten, to Gerard's pleasure, that he does not know how to drive.

"Boy, you're getting jowly, Jerry. Just like Daddy did."

"I really have to get back in time for morning prayers," he says.

"Are you sure?"

Even one night in his sister's house was more unpalatable than anything else he could think of. "I just wanted to know Trevor was okay."

"Alright." She yawns. She follows him to the door.

"Thank you for bringing him back," she says. She hugs him then, something she has never done before, not even at their parents' funerals.

Gerard steps outside into the frigid air. He heads back to the van and sits in the passenger side. He wonders what he should do. The gas station down the street may have a pay phone he could use to call the monastery, but he remembers hearing on television that pay phones are a thing of the past. Everyone has cell phones now. He takes the cell phone from the glove compartment. He recognizes the numbers zero through nine, but surrounding them is a mass of incomprehensible buttons. He puts it away again.

He glances around the parking lot. Lights are on in a few of the windows of the apartment building. He wonders how he might contact the residents. He could go to the lobby door, but just as with the cell phone, he has no way of telling which button to press.

Then he hears crying—the crying of a child. It's the baby in the back of the car next to him, still strapped into its car seat and struggling to break free. The young mother, who had only appeared to be sleeping, has thrown up on herself. Still unconscious, she is coughing, maybe choking.

Gerard hops out of the van and knocks on her window. The baby cries louder. He tries the car door, but it's locked. He jumps back into the van and retrieves the cell phone. It is the same jumble of buttons as before, but somehow he is able to focus on just one, one with a symbol representing an old-fashioned phone receiver. He presses it, and the entire phone seems to light up. He puts the phone to his ear and hears a dial tone. He dials 911.

It seems like a long time before an ambulance and a Boston police car show up, but in reality it is less than a minute.

The young woman at the wheel is lain out on a stretcher and loaded into the ambulance. The baby is put into the police car by one of the cops. The other one knocks at Gerard's window. Gerard has to get out of the van to talk to him, since the windows are electric.

The officer takes note of Gerard's robe. "You the one who called this in?" he says.

"Yes."

"You know her?" the cop says.

"No."

"What are you doing at this building at this time of night?" the cop wants to know. His voice takes on a skeptical edge that unnerves Gerard.

"My nephew...he was driving..."

"This building is known as a hub of drug activity."

Gerard does not respond.

"You probably saved her life," the cop says. He looks at the side of the van. "St. Bonaventure's?"

"That's my monastery."

"Yeah, I know it. I had an uncle who was a monk there. Long time ago."

The cop walks back to his cruiser and talks with the other officer while the ambulance pulls out and heads off. There is no siren.

Gerard gets back into the van. After a minute, the cops get into their cruiser. They drive off with a small wave.

Gerard wraps himself in his robe. Faintly, he smells bread. His surroundings seem to dissolve, and for hours he cannot move except to say, "Yes" and "I see" and "I love you so much."

Clifford Browder

DEEPER THAN THE ROOTS OF MEMORY

It is all around us if we listen
and inside us,
deeper than the roots of memory.

It can't be priced or packaged,
carved or counted,
bought or sold.
It's simply there; it exists.

It can heal and nourish, haunt, and terrify.

The home of thought and prayer—
It is close to us yet distant,
intimate, immense.
I have found it
in the secret places of my hiking,
in desolate dawns, temples of trees, breadth of sky.

As we work through
our spurts of joy and woe
and the grind of our clattering existence,
it waits for us—
A thief, an executioner,
a loving mother.

Silence:
Our origin, our home.

Kelly Jean White

TWO BIRDS IN FLAME

127. Shaker stove, cast iron, Enfield
*   moderate use, 17" high by 38" long, $550*

We've six months of winter, always. Snow
on the pumpkins on the vine in September,
the great ice storm this year, February 7th
with heavy limbs cracking like gunshots through
the night and morning. Today, April 17th
and snowing. A good six inches since
day break, and we're still two hours to nightfall.

Just yesterday I walked to the herb garden
with a light jacket and bare hands. I had been
delighted by the first bits of green breaking
through our rich soil. Today, snow clicked
sharp against my face when I went out for wood.
I admit the flakes were pretty against my new green
mittens, though I had not intended to wear them
this year, to find them pilled with snow when I brushed
off the woodpile. We've still enough wood. Providence

has provided us with forests, but we will always need
more for the more than eighty stoves in the Village. In
the Meeting House, the Dwellings, the Shops,
the Dining Hall, the Trustee's Office, and the Laundry
and Kitchen, each stove with its own need for wood.

I will lay my frozen mittens on the stove in
the Sister's Shop, taste the smell of boiling wool,
and feel my hands ache with returning color.
Sister Edith is certain to be closest to the stove
in the Shop or the Dwelling, or even in the
Meeting House. She dozes. Sometimes,

I'm tempted to let her lean a little too close to
the hot iron stove. But that is unkind, and she
is kind. Oh, April! I look forward to the True Spring.
To the arrival of lambs and calves, of kittens in the barn.
Like all creatures, may we be born anew this Spring.

Kimberly White

WORDS ON A STRING THEORY

There are no words for you

I had to borrow from the language of birds
to capture the contours of your face
to frame your cheeks and chin
with slither sounds
of wings that have brushed mountaintops

It was the language of trees
that explained how far you would go
to convince me to sink my feet
into your waters

You know you will drown me
at the very first chance

Only the language of fire
could convey the impact of your hands
shaping granite and water
with the same touch you use
on me or the sun

The whispered words of spiders
unlock the way you weave
stories, set my head on spin
for centuries

concurrent with the howls of stray cats
who roam silent night streets
wander in between alleys
criss-cross the ways you say you follow

when it is not night and not yet day

Guttural sounds of deep sea fish
whose light comes from
imagined eyes tell me they imagine you
as a shadow they cannot fathom
light definable only by your absence

I had to learn from the language of time
to diffuse the pitfalls I faced
following in your tracks

Only the hairshirt of belief
could break my dependence
on seeking your scent
with the blind hope of a pilgrim
on a rampage after God

but these words do not know you

These words cannot paint you
with the colors I see when my eyes
are closed and my fingers twitch on the
pulse of ripening earth

These words don't feel you as I do
in nerve endings that extend
beyond perimeters of flesh
deep into other worlds

impenetrable by sound
evolved beyond light
and gone before
we can form the word

blink

Edward Bruce Bynum

AFTER THE RAIN

After the rain has washed the dust away,
washed the heat away,
washed the morning away,
perfect hands come out of new air,
rearranging bushes, drying stems,
pulling concentration out of certain blue flowers.

The road ribbons out
speaking new cars, new smells,
bright windowpanes, ozone,
bursts of clear water
shaken from trees. There are
wheels with cool grease on them,
sacraments of wood.
Irises practice opening
on the paths you walk.

It is as though someone had been executed,
the bones washed away by the river,
as if we had lived through the death of
a religious tyrant, were free again
to inhabit god directly, in our own way.

For moments after this
each step is an original adventure,
each eye blinks a recording of something newer,

greener, more wet and succulent
than imagined before.
Dressed in forgiveness,
willing to fail, you launch
out of harbors where you had been held
by maps of what you thought you knew.

A black bird on a gravestone glistens,
caws, suggests you pass on.
Behind you, the trails thicken,
filling with spirits, noises, loss.

Jamie Donohoe

CAMPFIRE GODDESS

She exhumes Janis Joplin
and croons gravel-throated
folk tunes while we unravel
grateful smiles and gloat
the miles traveled, trail hike tales—
who chased the most coyotes,
the glistening things we've seen
and will yet see—and half-listen
to the rowdy boisterings
of proud tired day packers
sun-cheeked, red with weather
and glee, full of the memories
we'll exhume in all
the miles we'll travel soon.
It's true: Her songs will end
never, packed away in spaces
not readily seen, in our small
crevasses, beneath the river's curls
between ice and earth,
and the roots below:
This buried song we all share.
It's what fills the looming still
and the loneliness we find there.

Jamie Donohoe

ZIPPER TAG

In Zipper Tag you hunt
within the boundaries of a meadow;
to attack an opponent, touch the back and
tug down, making a drooping sound
like a falling cartoon moon:
Your opponent will slump over
as if you've just removed their spine.
If you are so inclined, you can zip up
slumpers with an upside-down ripping
motion, hands moving from back to nape;
then they can rejoin the hunt
until only one remains.

We played in teams of two, then four,
and before we left the slush-soaked meadow
full of tree debris and snowy saplings
we played a round of free-for-all;
with huffy laughter we spun and parried:
Watching your back is tough when
hands are clutching from every side.

This unhinged collide-a-scope flurried,
then subsided as we came
unzipped; the slumpers watched
the last survivors dart and spin
a booted ballet, slosh-stumping,

shrieking through sun and thick shadows
until a hand caught the last stumbler's back
and unzipped her, leaving the last man
standing in a ring of scattered spineless trees.

Before anybody could say "he's won,"
he quickly moved about and one by one
zipped us up.

 And with a gleeful hush
the meadow broke into a silence
that held us, like a long breath
before a snort of joy escapes your lungs,
and we exploded into the hunt again,
spilling, chasing, friend after friend,
and the game went on and on.

Robert Hirschfield

KATHMANDU MORNING

Annapurna's peaks
are on sale today in shops
all over Kantipath.

What do the trekkers seek
on the roof of the Alobar,
diddling numbered squares, tumbling West
through the chewed and scalloped air?

A *sadhu* lifts a dust planet
from his dark toenail.

In Kathmandu, God is easier to find
than a traffic light.

Jennifer Raha

PEDIGREE

What we haul is reclamation,
no plunder, no pillage—

restoration, the taking back
of what was rendered.

Parents, grandparents, we envy.
Our days are not of the Depression

but the Regression, bodies
inflated with hope, like balloons.

From Kennedy to Obama,
we believed this revival. But

our accounts are an annex, seized.
Loans grip our neck at night.

What do we have to conquer
in our new colony?

We, the bellhops and hired hands.
What portion is rationed for us?

Tim Bascom

CONSIDER THE RAVENS

SINCE THE HARVEST IS NEARLY DONE here in southern Ethiopia, all the farmers and wives have come to the dirt field in the center of the village to lay their wares on the ground: pyramids of ripening papayas, cellophane sacks of coffee beans, pots of home-churned butter, chickens trussed at the feet, little sheaves of chickpeas on the branch, and bags and bags of winnowed *teff* ready to be trucked to Addis where they can be sold to rich city women for their *injera* crepes. All of the people milling around—barefoot and dressed in homespun cotton—make this market day feel like something straight out of the *Bible*. They might as well be gathered on the outskirts of ancient Jerusalem, haggling over dried dates or doves or lambs for the altar.

With all the hubbub, no one notices a thirteen-year-old boy squatting outside the crowd. He is of no importance there under the mango sapling, sitting on his heels in earth-brown shorts and a ragged sweater. It would seem he is just another dusty farm boy keeping an eye on the family donkey.

A gang of townies, unencumbered by chores, plays football beside the market square, kicking a sphere of plastic bags wrapped in twine, and the boy watches closely, wishing he was their friend. To be more specific, he wishes he was playing.

One of them shouts, "Hey, let's see if my mother will give us some *kolo* or sugar cane."

Squatting there, the boy thinks that his whole future could change if he just got into this game. Maybe his days would click into place like beads on a rosary.

People would finally take notice and give him their support, all because he could out-juke the others, becoming, for a moment, someone worth noticing

He can smell the food all around him—the pungent odor of ripening bananas and the savory burn of chili pepper—which nearly makes him swoon. How could he play well if he hasn't eaten since yesterday, when his uncle told him to put down his bread and get to work?

The threshing floor was not smooth enough for the short, rock-faced man, who did not want a single crack where loose grain might catch. So the boy had to return to work, spreading another layer of dung. It was out there, kneeling on the threshing floor with a handful of wet manure, that he decided, like lightning, to run away. He would not stay another minute with this tyrant of an uncle, even if leaving meant losing the last link to his dead mother.

I'm destined for better—that's what he told himself as he washed his hands at the creek and started up the mountain trail. Hadn't his mother always said so? Hadn't she boasted, before she got sick, that he could end up as famous as the boy-king Yekuno Amlak, whose mother had hidden him in a monastery after the prophet predicted he would take the throne? With faith, anything was possible, right?

And so here he is. A very-hungry kid who has hiked alone over two full mountains, sleeping overnight under a bush. A kid who is operating on pure belief, even praying as he squats in the afternoon shade, pinching his nostrils against the stomach-cramping aromas of food.

No one glances in his direction. Instead, their attention swings to a hefty white foreigner who has arrived in a Land Cruiser and waded into the crowd, ushered by a minister from the new evangelical church. This pale bald-headed foreigner is a dentist and a Baptist elder in Nebraska, and he is here for a short-term medical mission. He has been doing root canals all week, ticking them off like a list of extra-credit assignments. He's not all business, though. He figures he deserves a bit of a holiday, so he has borrowed a car and a driver from the missionaries who run the clinic, and he is taking a two-night trip to visit a game park.

The only reason for this late-afternoon stop is that the missionaries have asked him to drop off their locally trained minister. In fact, the visiting Nebraskan would still be in the Land Cruiser if it were not for the pastor's convincing him to take a peek inside his recently built church.

Despite the delay, the visiting dentist is feeling good. It's obvious. His vague smile says he enjoys all the children calling out "Ferengi" and the men staring suspiciously, not to mention the shy women glancing up from their stacks of vegetables, as if he were a singing minstrel. Back home, he has never made such a splash.

He stops halfway across the dirt square to shake hands with several introduced church members. He greets each with a traditional "Tenahstehlin," trying to mean it in the way he's heard it translated: "May God give you health."

As for our unremarkable thirteen-year-old, he is still squatting in the shade, staring as the soccer players break off their game to tag along behind the foreigner. While they grin and whisper, amused by the strangeness of his accent, the hungry boy watches, his wide eyes intense. Then, he stands and moves toward the crowd, taking a true step of faith. He has decided that this stranger's appearance could be the sign he has been looking for since running away—the sign that his fortune will finally change for the better.

He thinks in such a fashion, because before his mother died two years ago, she used to tell him stories about saints. She used to tell him especially about Gabra Manfas Qeddus, praising him on fasting days, and the boy's favorite tale was the one about an angel carrying Qeddus into the desert, where the transported man grew hair all over his body and walked safely among lions and leopards. This is what he's looking for now: either an angel or a miracle.

However, the American strolls along, entirely unaware of such yearnings. He pauses at a platter of flat bread that an elderly lady is selling with boiled coffee. "What is this?" he asks in English, pointing to the thin glutinous squares.

"It is our Ethiopian bread," the minister explains.

"You mean *injera*?"

The minister shakes his tightly sheared head. "A different bread. *Enset*. From the roots and plant of the false banana. It is the poor man's bread. You want to try?"

The Nebraskan is not interested. He waves a hand in refusal. But the minister is already asking the old woman, in Amharic, if she will give the foreigner a bite.

She laughs, putting a hand over the toothless gap in her mouth. Then, she lifts a square of the flat gray stuff.

The boy salivates, watching. Wouldn't it be nice to have a piece? In fact, he thinks, "If I just believe, believe, believe—like Gabra Manfas Qeddus—then maybe this foreigner will give a piece of bread to me, ask my name, and offer to be my patron for the rest of this life."

Surprisingly, the visiting dentist does turn toward the boy, but his gaze slides over the youth's shoulder and settles on a fat baby a mother is holding, to whom he offers the remaining *enset*.

Now, as the thirteen-year-old follows along, all knobby knees and chapped hands, doubt begins to shadow him, prowling on ghostly feet. The boy is disturbed by the thought that he must not have shown enough faith. Otherwise, the visitor would surely have seen him, would have felt the nudge of God. He winces as he trails along.

THE MINISTER AND THE AMERICAN reach the entrance of the church, where the minister unlocks the padlock. Then, all of the curious children scatter, afraid to enter a place their parents don't trust. This is not a proper Orthodox Church with octagonal walls and a pillared entrance. It does not have loudspeakers on poles to broadcast the morning prayer, or a priest with a white turban.

However, the hungry boy has no guardian to stop him. Even if he has begun to falter, he has nothing left to lose, so he follows a few feet behind the two men and steps into the sanctuary.

He listens closely now, although he cannot understand the English words the minister is using: "After we are done singing, can you speak a few words?"

"You mean today? Right now?"

"Just a short message of encouragement."

"Look, I didn't even know there was a service."

The minister grimaces, caught between an apology and a reaction. "No service. Only a few words. I told people you were bringing a greeting."

It is unsettling how quiet everything gets as the American absorbs what he has heard. People are expecting him to stay and speak. The silence them extends as he considers his options.

The kid nearly blows it. He wants to take a step forward now and ask for help; however, he knows that this could be a mistake.

He has seen adults turn cruel when they are nervous or frustrated. With his uncle, it didn't matter how small the problem. If the batteries in the radio went dead, the man had to hit something. He'd kick the goat or smack the boy.

The American frowns. "I am not trained to preach," he tells the minister.

He is brittle now, because he is bothered about more than the church service. He is worrying about the odd-tasting bread he hadn't wanted to eat out there in the market square, the bread gummy in his mouth, as if not baked, sitting on a dusty platter with flies. Now, there is this second imposition, which makes him want to jog right back to the Land Cruiser. Why is it that Ethiopians are always ambushing him with public formalities? If he were back at the tourist hotel in Arba Minch, he could eat something safe and retire to a private room. He could read a trashy thriller and drink a beer with no one forming judgments.

Carefully, he reins in his reaction. He tries to play the role he's been assigned. "Okay, just a short message. Nothing fancy."

For a moment, the minister isn't sure he understands. Seeing the stiffness in the other man's smile, he asks, "Is it okay?"

"Gidelem," replies the American, remembering the Amharic term for "no problem."

"But you need to tell the driver, so he knows I will be staying a bit."

There's a slight turn in the mood after this surprising resolution, as if the air has lightened after a storm. The boy senses the change, even though he can't understand any of what the two men have said—nothing except for an English word that he learned at school, before his mother died and his uncle made him stop attending.

"Okay." That's the word, and it makes sense now—alive with its fundamental meaning—because he can see that some sort of agreement has transpired. Maybe everything really will be "okay" he hopes, as he takes a step forward.

Abruptly, the minister turns, frowning. "Mindino?" he demands, wanting to know what the boy is after.

"Nothing, sir," the boy answers in Amharic. "Just maybe some food."

"Ah beit. This is not a restaurant. If you want to worship, sit down. Otherwise, you must leave."

The boy is not surprised by this brusque response. He nods timidly and moves to the end of a bench. He is working on the assumption that, if he just endures, one of these two men might take pity. They have resolved their own problem, whatever it was, so maybe they will resolve his, too.

He tries not to look interested as the American makes another comment in English: "I can stay only a short while. Right? Just thirty minutes. So you need to tell the driver."

"No worries," replies the minister. "Short, short. I promise." And he jogs out to the driver, not giving the boy another glance.

After that, the little adobe church is quiet, with the big dentist and the dusty boy thinking their own separate thoughts. The tin creaks, cooling in the waning sunlight. The dentist sits on a bench near the podium, picking his teeth. What should he use as a focus for his impromptu sermon? Without a Bible, he can only rely on verses he knows by heart.

"In the beginning was the Word, and the Word was with God..." No, too abstract.

"For the wages of sin are death, but the gift of God is eternal life." Better, but pretty much an altar-call, which might get too involved.

The boy sits patiently. He studies the interior of the church, noting all that is unfamiliar. No red or gold drapes to mark the holy of holies. No brocaded umbrellas for the priest to carry in procession. Not even a bronze cross on a staff, like he has seen at the church his uncle sometimes attends. Just a podium and an open book—a mysterious book that is elevated as if it were more important than anything else.

The foreignness of the space makes him feel like any move he makes could be wrong, but he fears this might be his only chance to interact with the American. Finally, he risks approaching. Wordless, he pads to the front of the church and, for a full minute, watches the man staring at his clasped hands.

"Hello," whispers the boy, remembering this unexpected English word.

The American shakes his head.

The boy tries again. "Hello."

And this time the American glances up with a scowl. "Look, I need to concentrate," he says.

The boy furrows his brow, not able to understand. He senses the man's flagging attention, so he lifts his fingers, pinching them together like the beak of a bird. Then, he pokes at his mouth.

The man frowns harder and pats his pockets, holding his hands out empty.

The boy tilts his head and lifts his fingers again, beak-like, so that he can poke at his lips. The gesture is so pathetic that he knows it has to have an impact at some basic level. At the same time, it is completely unsatisfactory. There is so much more he would say if he could, such as, "Yes, I want food. But I also have no family. I am a runaway. I am hoping for someone like you to become my sponsor. I need you to give me a room and bed. I will be good. I will do chores. I just want to go to school. If you will help me go to school, you won't be sorry. I promise. I'll work very hard and become something remarkable. My mother said I would."

The American pats his pockets again, turning one of them inside out. He shrugs and looks over the boy's shoulder, having noticed that people are drifting in.

The boy steps a foot closer. Too late, though. The minister is back, dashing up the aisle, and the kid is forced to turn away, slumping into a back pew. At this point, he doesn't want to consider his options. Does he have the strength to walk back over two mountain ranges to his uncle's house? Or would he drop, to be picked apart by crows? These thoughts are uneasy shadows in his mind, swirling and trying to take shape.

The minister stands and says, "Initsully," but the boy stays seated—too disconsolate to join into the opening prayer. He hardly hears anything as the minister murmurs to God, as he pauses and begins to sing, lifting his arms to invite the congregation into call-and-response.

Only when it is time to introduce the foreign speaker—"Doctor Emerson from Nebraska, United States"—does the boy look up.

The thick-set dentist slowly approaches the podium, where the waiting reverend is preparing to translate. Then, he raises his straw-colored eyebrows, as if shaking off drowsiness, and leaps into a barely-formed sermon.

"Today, I feel called to talk to you about something we all struggle with. Whether we live in Ethiopia or America, we all know about this problem. We all know how to worry. Take me. Even before standing up here, I was worried about what to say to you. I was not prepared to speak. But that is when a special verse came to me: 'Consider the ravens. They do not sow or reap, they have no storehouse or barn; yet God feeds them.'"

The boy can see that the foreigner wants to surge on, swept by his oratory, but the minister has interrupted to translate more fully. The thin, stern man flips back and forth in an Amharic *Bible* until he finds the right passage—"Then Jesus said to his disciples, 'Therefore I tell you, do not worry about your life, what you will eat; or about your body, what you will wear. Life is more than food, and the body more than clothes. Consider the ravens: they do not sow or reap, they have no storeroom or barn; yet God feeds them.'"

Impatient, the American leaps back into his message. He explains that his own family was—though it might surprise everyone—quite poor.

The hungry boy struggles to follow the galloping translation, thrown off by foreign words and gestures. He has trouble concentrating because part of him is still back at the quoted verses, pondering one sentence in particular: "Do not worry about your life." For him, it is as if God has read his mind, seeing the anxiety that lay there. Maybe, God has finally noticed.

While the American dentist goes on describing how his dad, a poor handyman, never had enough money to buy a car, the boy shivers with wonder, amazed by the aptness of this Bible passage. Yes, he thinks, it must be meant for me. It is too perfect to be coincidence. At last, a sign.

On goes the dentist, trying to explain how, in America, every family has a car, which means it can be embarrassing not to have a car. He says he used to feel ashamed of having to walk to the grocery store in winter when there was ice all over the ground. All of the normal, sane people were in their heated sedans or pick-ups. But him? He was out there skating on the sidewalks.

The Ethiopian minister has to break in now, asking for help translating unfamiliar words like "sedan" or "grocery" or "skating." The story becomes fractured. However, the visiting American powers on, gaining confidence because he can see fascination building on the faces of his congregation—people who are trying to imagine a place where everyone has a car and buys food at a single large store and falls down because there is ice sheeting the ground.

"I used to feel so ashamed," says the American, "that I'd leave the house early on Sunday mornings, so I wouldn't have to walk with the family. I'd go down the alleyways, hoping to avoid everyone. I did that all the way through grade school. Then, guess what? One of the elders from our church realized that my family walked everywhere—that my father even had to walk to his jobs—and he told my dad he would sell him a used car for only a dollar."

Hearing that, people begin to murmur. Wow, wouldn't that be something. To get a usable car for a dollar. To ride down the road, instead of walking or swaying on a mule. But the boy at the back is still stuck on his own line of thought.

Is God actually talking to me? Will it all turn out okay if I just live like a raven?

He is starting to bank on those verses, deciding that maybe, if he really believes this time, not allowing any doubt to creep in—not the slightest bit—then maybe, God will honor his faith. Maybe, God has been waiting to see if he will show complete trust like his hero Gabra Manfas Qeddus.

The amazing thing is that this kid has never seen an actual raven. A crow, yes, but not a real raven with its four-foot-wide wing span.

The only raven he's heard about is the evil one his mom used to describe in one of her Qeddus stories—a well-worn tale about the saint going on a walkabout after completing his monastery studies in the crater of Zuqulla. It's the story of Qeddus' stopping to stare straight up into heaven for seven months—so long, in fact, that the devil became enraged and descended as a big black bird to peck out his eyes.

Raven as devil, or raven as God's chosen creature? That's the dilemma. And after hearing about the wicked version, it's hard for the kid to think that ravens could be good creatures, cared for by God. After all, Qeddus could have spent the rest of his life blind, if it wasn't for the angels who healed him. It's amazing that yet the boy can imagine himself as a raven—trying to take each moment as its own moment, worrying about nothing.

As he sits there, he begins to think he can feel something different in his bones—an airy lightness, a sense that he could fly. He begins to trust that God will give him what he needs—if only he believes.

THE SERMON ENDS AND THE MINISTER says a prayer and, when people stand, the boy feels a breeze pass through the meeting hall. He shivers as they start to move toward the doorway, shaking hands.

As for the Nebraskan dentist, he is flushed with warmth because he has done "the right thing," even though it took extra effort. He relishes the way the local church members bow as they touch his hand. He is inspired by their humility, not at all aware of the dusty boy in baggy shorts, until he realizes that someone is standing aside from the greeting line. With a start, the Nebraskan realizes this is the same kid who had accosted him before the service, pointing to his lips. He is surprised that the youth is no longer begging—that he even seems at peace, grinning as if he holds a you-can-never-guess secret.

Happy not to be pestered, the dentist feels generous suddenly. He wonders if he should do something. Maybe, give the boy something. But what? He can't pull out his wallet in public.

There is a water bottle in the man's hand, almost empty, and he recalls how the driver of his Land Cruiser tossed a finished bottle to a child when they stopped on the roadside earlier. Perhaps, the empty bottle could be of use. He holds the plastic bottle out, putting it into the hand of the boy. He gives him some good eye contact, too, before stepping out into the dusky marketplace, where the sun has set, and the vendors are packing away their goods. He quick-walks across the market square toward the waiting Land Cruiser. He is sure that he deserves his long-delayed holiday and slides into the car, ready to order a beer, to read that trashy thriller.

A few moments later, the minister comes out, padlocking the church. He is humming, because five newcomers have come to hear the visiting preacher. Five potential new members. He jingles the keys in his pocket as he strolls away, noticing only a few people scattered across the darkening grounds. Among the silhouetted figures is a boy about twelve or thirteen who is leaning against a post.

Not until the minister has reached the main road does he realize that this is the same kid who came into the church asking for food. He has never seen that boy before today, which makes him hesitate, considering whether he should turn back and ask where the youth lives, but he is too exhausted. He has taken an early morning bus, gone to the mission bookstore to ask about a set of hymnals, gone to the printer to see why the books weren't printed, then traveled back with the American doctor and organized this unexpected service. He knows his wife will be wondering why he has not come home, so he flips on his flashlight and keeps moving.

Alone, the boy is left with his remaining scrap of faith. He pushes away a pang of fear. Consider the ravens, he thinks.

He drinks the tiny bit of water in the plastic bottle. It tastes chemical, and he feels removed from the foreigner rather than close. The bottle is light in his hand, completely empty, so he drums it against the post by his side.

There is one other person on the dark stage of this emptied marketplace, a bent woman gathering her wares. For a bit, the boy tries not to notice her as he waits and drums his water bottle. He wants to stand here the way a raven would stand in a field— without even the need for hope. Whatever happens must happen from outside him now. How else will he know whether it comes from God?

Then—as this last person straightens, lifts her stool and bags, turns to shuffle away—the boy is done with his hard, hard experiment. Panic rises up inside him, causing his legs to quiver as he sprints toward her, feet slapping on the dust.

"Tesfaye, is that you?" calls the old woman. Then she sucks in her breath: "Ah beit. I thought you were my neighbor's child. Who are you?"

"Yohannes."

This is the same woman who gave the square of *enset* to the American. Despite his distress, Yohannes recognizes her by the gap where her upper teeth ought to be.

She glances around as if he might be hiding the correct boy.

He knows he is about to be dismissed, and this time he doesn't bother to pray. Whatever happens, it must be up to him.

He opens his lips and blurts, "Please, ma'am, can you give me something to eat? I can work. I will carry your things if I can just have something to eat."

The old woman stares at this twelve or thirteen year old boy named Yohannes, trying to make out his features in the dim light. She sighs. "Come. If you will take these bags, I will give you some bread."

He lifts her two cloth bags—one on each side, heavy with the clay pot, the platter of remnant bread, the *enset* leaves that she uses for wrapping. He is relieved to be with someone, but there is nothing magical about this moment, not the way he had envisioned it would be.

The moment is really quite ordinary—like spreading dung on a threshing floor.

He thinks the world will never be the same for him. How can it be? Or maybe, it will always be the same.

He feels earthbound as he follows the old woman into the dark—unlike the raven he had imagined. He is held down by his unspoken past and the weight of what is yet unknown. These weights are heavier than the yoke his uncle used to make him lug from the river with buckets of water. Nevertheless, when the old woman turns onto an unfamiliar path, shuffling into the darker shadows, Yohannes adjusts the bags in his grip and follows. He feels his way along, barely able to see the flicker of a distant lamp.

Jody Azzouni

THIS DOESN'T BELONG TO YOU

"ACTUALLY, I DON'T LIKE CATS," she tells her boss. "Because cats are sneaks."

"Um," her boss says. He often says *um*. Sometimes, he says more. Like now.

"When people are hungry," her boss says, "they steal. They take bribes."

"Not everyone does that," she says. "My parents were starving. Lots of times they were starving. They never take nothing from no one. They will die first."

"Um," her boss says. He gestures at a table. "Those people over there," he says, "they're ready for you. They've closed their menus."

She rushes over to take their order.

Then, she moves on to the next table.

This man is always smiling when he comes in. He's always flirting with her. In a nice way. He's an older man. A little older than she is.

"He's famous," she gushes to her boss, who nods without smiling. "He has his own Wikipedia entry. Gardner, his name is Kevin Gardner." It's a good name, she thinks. Also, his name, Kevin, is popular in America. He's a writer, like Shevchenko. He comes in to get coffee almost every morning, with his Kindle under his arm.

Kevin tells her everywhere he's been invited to speak. Paris. Budapest. Rome. The usual places. That's what he says. And he shows her something he's written. "Those are footnotes," he tells her, which annoys her because she already knows what footnotes are.

"The footnotes are there so that people will know you didn't steal the idea, that you're willing to give the person who came up with it the credit. Even if they're dead and don't care."

She nods, looking into his eyes. She can do that now, without feeling uncomfortable.

"You have beautiful eyes," he says. More than once.

Every girl has beautiful eyes, she thinks. That's what makeup is for.

"Coffee? Or dinner? Lunch?" That's what he asks her this particular time, after telling her again about her eyes.

She shakes her head no, looking away. She never looks into his face when she tells him no. Not even to tell him, "No, we don't have blueberry muffins, today. Sorry." Or "No. No lunch, no dinner, no coffee. No."

"He's cute," she tells her boss. "I hope he meets someone like him."

"Um," her boss says.

No milk. Again. Her boss isn't there, and people get so mad when there's no milk.

"Kevin," she says, using his name. He looks up from his book. They're the only ones in the café at the moment. "I need to get some milk," she tells him. "They didn't deliver it, again. Watch the counter for me."

"Why?" he asks. "The milk people had something more interesting to do?"

She's laughing as she runs out the door.

"Are you ready?" she asks.

Her boss is standing next to her as she takes the order. Something he never does. "I have to show you something," he says.

He runs the tape, and she sees Kevin behind the counter. He's stealing a muffin.

Her boss points his finger emphatically when he's stressing a point. The gesture reminds her of being in church. "He's rich, this guy," the boss says, pointing his finger at her. "He's famous like you said he is, so he doesn't have to steal. Why would a rich, famous person have to steal a muffin from us?"

She googles him. Carefully this time. Really looking. She finds a blogger who accuses him of plagiarism. She's pretty sure it's the same guy. Kevin Gardner. Some nineteenth century book of poems or something. From Riga. Latvia. That's the book that he stole stuff from. It went out of print in 1926. The blogger suggests that maybe Kevin Gardner thought no one would notice.

"It doesn't make any sense," she texts her friend. "Why steal something like that? He knows there are cameras all over the place. Everyone knows that. What's wrong with him, he's stupid? And for an old muffin?"

"You're such an a-hole, and I thought you were a nice guy." That's what she says to him, when he comes in next. Right away, she says that.

"You can't talk to me that way," he says back. He looks mad.

But she can talk to him that way. "Leave this place, and don't come in again. You're not welcome, anymore."

He leaves. He really does, without saying anything else.

"Everyone makes mistakes." That's what she says to her boss later, after she's texted some of her friends, talked to a few neighbors, vented, told them all that she doesn't like anyone anymore.

"We shouldn't judge others." That's what she says to her boss, now.

"Um," the boss says.

"My girlfriend is a good girl," she tells her boss. "One of them I mean. She really is. But sometimes she cheats on her boyfriend. Goes out with someone else."

"Who's that?" the boss says. "I ever meet this friend of yours?"

"Nope," she says. "It's someone in Russia. Miles away." She glances at her boss. "You should find your own girl like that." Then, she's looking down at the counter, smiling to herself. She doesn't see her boss's expression.

"Some people are proud to think that they are good, but they just think they are good. There's nothing to be proud of." She tells her boss that, looking down at the counter. And then she brings an old couple their tea.

"If you're honest, maybe you don't do so well. In the world, I mean." Later she tells her boss this.

"Um," the boss says. Then he says, "Throw those muffins out, will you? They've been in the case way too long."

"COFFEE?" HE SAYS to her. He's come back in. After two weeks. Her boss is watching him. From the back. Maybe warily.

"Or dinner?" he adds. "To explain myself. Because I'm sorry. I don't know what I did, but I'm sorry anyway."

"Yes," she says.

"Yes?" he says. She hears in his voice that he can't believe she's just said yes, because she's not looking at him. She's looking down at the counter, smiling.

"Yes," she says again. "Yes."

George Held

HARAMBE, HARAMBE

O rare Silverback,
O mighty Harambe,
may your spirit
forgive the primates
who captured, bought and sold
you, shipped you from
Africa to Cincinnati,
and displayed you
in a "natural habitat,"
then executed you
without a trial,
with no brief for your
defense, but still,
your death might, as your
Swahili name suggests,
help us to "come together,"
to protect us from each other,
proving your seventeen years
of magnificent apehood
worth all the three-year-
old boys in the wide world,
O rare Silverback,
O great Harambe.

George Held

ISLE AND…

Island is land
amid ocean

Seeing eye land
where the one

eyed man's no
king; I'm king

of my mind's eye
land where

imagination
rules the island

nation; cloud
islands form sky's

archipelago
where the eye

reads shapes
and the mind

directs them
where to go.

Rich Murphy

THE STORAGE SHED

I think that means that instead of living under the sun and the moon and the sky and the stars, we're living in a fantasy world of our own making.
—Wallace Shawn

Inside the storage shed,
drafts whistle through the seams
at times, threatening to lift
clay pots from benches, and the versed
repair to fix feet to the floor.

Just outside,
where money reaps,
one by one the poor react as predicted
to the assaults, so that prison
or the cemetery await;

where the Palestinian chair,
water board, and sleep deprivation trigger,
inducing fantasy for American graduates;

where international schadenfreude
stands guard in the watch towers.

Further outside,
the spotlight
for the accidental freak show
ignores with mathematical accuracy,
allowing the science meme
to talk and walk with arrogance.

Once the contents rest on the curb
with the sign "Free" so to speak only,
two cheeks fill with apple sauce
from a spoon until the clinking
on the bowl falls silent.

Haley Guariglia

PHENOMENA

1800 miles from heart of things I courted
sand, scoured hidden and folic depressions.
I pilfered gold with a boat neck while morning
tide paraded up and down the beach.

Back at my apartment, we sat missing
cushion backs, watching the absence
of television programs, the harsh brow.

After hours we pressed each other
against glass at Thuan Phat,
named five live bullfrogs and left.

We washed one another slowly,
bare apertures eroding.
Sand drained down me.
The gaping horizon, stark red
welt, etched whisper, gone.

Tim Robbins

AFTER ORLANDO

Walk to the CVS reading of
a long-dead Chinese bride
who snubs her mother-in-law:
The first taste of soup goes to
her husband's sister,
the only in-law who liked her.

In '78 there was only Hooks
Drug Store in a town so
sheltered no one noticed
the ominous name. I learned
this when a touch woke the
least tangible ghost and left
me inert. I was looking for
men with cheeks dinted like
the sides of a cowboy hat
and hands that do feats as
though playing a pedal steel
guitar. A car engine turning
over at the start of a trip.

Mom clears her throat
before launching into Brad's
boys—one a schizophrenic
who adores all drugs but
his antipsychotics and the other

a tenor freshman at Massillon
Baptist College. Brad says
one is too heavy to carry,
the other too light.

Further south on TV
mother and son share a face:
round smiles and beaver
incisors. They share a
name: Christ-follower and
Christ-bearer. I scour the
web for his friends' names.
Their anonymity becomes
their beauty, as they flank
his mother, rubbing her arms
as though the grief is in her
triceps—as she once rubbed
dirt from her slain son's cheek.
Their dark lashes would fan
her if they had the power.

Moses and Elijah,
they rise from the convention
floor. Good news lights
up the teleprompter. The son's
final choreographic gift:
letting his mom carry him
up the street to the trauma center.

Greg Moglia

SORRY

Down the steps to my train, a stranger is a step ahead.
I brush her side. *Sorry* she says, and I think, *Another sorry.*

In the market I wait while a woman reaches for a can of tuna.
She turns…sees me says *Sorry*, and I mutter *It's ok.*

Sorry…sorry all the women shopping away.
*Sorry…*why? I think *'sorry-making machines.'*

The 'sorries' point at me, and I've no place to hide.
I see my daughter at my den door.

Daddy, I need a band-aid.
And me cursing *Damn, I just lost my thought.*

And she with *Sorry, Daddy, but I'm bleeding.*

J.R. Townley

ALL THAT GLITTERS

I KILL MY INDIAN DOWN THE ROAD, then trudge up the path toward the cabin. Pines and giant sequoias creak as they sway in the mountain breeze. Unseen birds twitter, wings aflutter. I struggle to muffle the clang of my armor. Surprise is my only weapon, besides my flintlock and sword.

Smoke billows from the chimney, and this means only one thing: Someone's guarding the gold.

I have a plan. I always have a plan. You can't just waltz in and ask for the hoard. After all, these days, everyone's armed, and much progress has been made in the realm of weaponry since I was issued my first sidearm.

So, I creep around to the backdoor, a hundred percent stealth. I climb the three steps, then sidle across a large redwood deck. I'm preparing to brandish my sword, kick in the door, and proclaim my demands in a most stentorian voice, when I hear the telltale chambering of shells in a pump-action shotgun. I think immediately of the Jackson, Tennessee hoard, then clench my teeth and fight off a surge of fear. Thirty years was yesterday, and the wounds still sting.

"Not so fast, buckethead."

Hand on the hilt of my steel, I turn to face a woman—a woman—brandishing a 12-gauge. Worse, she looks like an Indian. Worse still, she has ambushed me.

"You will surrender your weapon," I say, "atone for your insult, and pay fealty to your new master."

"Fat chance, twinkle toes," she says, smirking.

At least I know I've come to the right place.

"Now, I'll only say this once before I start shooting," she says. "Get off my property, and don't come back. There's nothing for you here. Got it?"

With one swing of my sword, I could slaughter the savage. I would first cut off her arms, then her legs, then her head, then open her abdomen and rip out her entrails, just as I was taught to do so many years ago. Only I don't have the heart for it. Or the stomach. I've always been too squeamish for this business.

I need a new plan.

"Please forgive me. We got up on the wrong leg."

"Got off on the wrong foot."

"Exactemente."

She covers half the distance between us, then turns me toward the steps. "Get marching, or I'll blow both your feet off."

She blasts a shot into the sky, scaring birds from their perches. She may even have hit a squirrel. I wince and bite my lip.

Ears ringing, I say, "I am called Juan Francisco Hernán Vásquez de Léon."

"That's a mouthful."

I should throw her to the ground, choke her into submission, and have my way with her. We take no flak from those we conquer. Instead, I say, "Please, call my Vásquez. All my friends do."

"Baskets? That figures. Anyway, we're not friends, remember? And you were just leaving."

By now, she's marched me off the deck and around to the front of the house.

"You are a very difficult woman," I say, chuckling though nothing is funny. "But I always get my way. I will not go into detail right now. Too gruesome for a lady, even a savage such as yourself."

I spit for dramatic flair. "But know this. I shall return for the gold which is rightfully mine."

"Whatever you say, Baskets." She grins without mirth, then pumps a new shell into the chamber. "You're always welcome."

I CLANG AND CLATTER DOWN THE PATH toward my Indian, though I have no intention of leaving. Not when I'm finally so close to realizing my life's work. After all this time, I can sense gold from miles away. The warm scent like baked earth and tree bark, the taste like flecks of spring sunshine, the heavy clink and rattle like nothing else on earth. So, I remove my chest protector and helmet, and stow my flintlock.

I wait for the night to deepen. Through the forest's dense silence comes a grinding moan that grows and swells. Soon, I make out two beams of light, and a hulking shadow passes up the road toward the cabin. I wait and listen. Doors are slamming, voices tinkling in the distance. Who it might be, I can only speculate. I must be patient. A short time later, the same shadow lurches back down the road, but something's different.

The hot glow of gold.

I pounce on the Indian's back, then kick him over and over again, but he will not go. "¡Hijo de puta!" I say in a muted shriek. "The gold is getting away." Then, the syrupy stench of gasoline— The engine's flooded. Under my breath, I whisper hateful insults about the Indian's mother, his breeding, his very race, but the steel horse is obdurate, refusing to obey my commands, as if prepared to suffer the ultimate sacrifice.

A sliver of moon lights my path as I creep back up to the cabin. In another time, I would've crashed through a window, then raped, tortured, and mutilated the savage until she told me what I wanted to know, the cabin going up in flames around us. It's textbook. We call it El Método, and the widely celebrated conquests of Ponce de León, Cortés, and Cabeza de Vaca, among others, attest to its efficacy. What it lacks in subtlety, it makes up for in showmanship. Anyway, as everyone knows, The Method's the quickest path to glory. Trouble is, it's never worked that well for me. Or perhaps I never mastered its nuances—just when to spark the flame, for instance, or how much information to sacrifice for carnage.

So, I wait in the darkness, listening for the creak of bedsprings, the moan of floorboards. My breath steams in the liquid moonlight, but I'm too focused now to feel the chill. When I'm confident the savage must be sleeping, I jimmy the lock on the backdoor, then slip into the cabin's musty warmth.

Cinders cool in the fireplace. The room smells of smoke and freshly baked bread. I slowly slip my sword from its scabbard, then creep toward the bedroom. I sense the savage before I make out her contours beneath the blankets. She's bathed in an eerie blue light that emanates from a small bulb near the floor. Although time is of the essence—my gold has escaped—I again force myself to be patient. I stand at the threshold and take one deep breath after another. When I'm still, calm, and focused, I cover the short distance to the bed, lay my steel across her neck, and say, "Now, you will tell me who has stolen my gold."

The savage is slow to awaken. I slap her gently. I do not like to repeat myself.

I repeat myself.

"If it isn't Baskets," she says. "Know something? Your breath reeks."

"You will beg my forgiveness for your loose tongue."

"Or what? You'll slit my throat?"

"That's the idea."

Her grin blooms in the dim, blue light. "But then how will you get the gold?"

I take a deep breath and count to ten, waiting for the surge of anger to subside. In another time, I would've lopped her head off with one quick stroke.

"I have other means of persuasion besides death."

"Such as?"

"Torture, mutilation, dismemberment."

"Meaning?"

"I could filet your feet," I offer. "Meaning I'd tie you down and slice your soles off, one layer at a time, until you told me what I wanted to know."

She shivers, I assume from fear and revulsion. "I didn't take you for a barbarian, Baskets. You'd actually do that?"

"I have years of practice, and I just sharpened my blade." I clear my throat. "Now you must tell me. Who came for my gold?"

"His name is Haege. He's a numismatist."

"¿Perdón?"

The savage mulls for a moment. "Like an appraiser and broker rolled into one."

"And where has this middleman taken my gold?"

"His office in San Francisco." She stares at me staring at her, perhaps realizes the gravity of her predicament. "Financial District."

"Fine," I say, nodding. "Now you shall take me to him."

Perhaps, she has some witty repartee, but she keeps it to herself. It's a good sign. I watch her carefully as she dresses, lest she use her savage cunning and disappear into the night. Measure twice, cut once, as Coronado always used to say. Then, we climb into her old Dakota and wind our way down the pitted gravel road to the valley below.

THE DRIVE TO SAN FRANCISCO IS LONG. The savage remains taciturn for the first hour; we both nod off. We're well over the center line and drifting toward a ditch when I start from a thick slumber. I grab the helm and right the ship, then force the savage over at the next Chandler's. We both load up on what they call coffee; it tastes of scorched earth and is so viscous I almost have to chew it.

After that, I feel like I'm going to jump out of my skin, but I keep refilling my cup from the thermos. For the rest of the drive, the savage talks a mile a minute. Mostly, she recounts a preposterous story about how she discovered my gold. She was walking a trail on Paradise Mountain, her ancestral land, thinking about her savage husband, a courier who died in a flaming highway accident. She spotted a rusty can, half-buried at the foot of a tree; it was full of coins. When she poked around in the same area, she found five more cans, all of them full of gold.

"Face value's only about $30,000," she explains. "But these are old coins, Baskets. Collector's items. Haege says they may bring ten or fifteen million when all's said and done."

"Foolish savage," I say, clucking my tongue.

The lights of Sacramento already shimmer behind us when she says, "Listen, Baskets, would you please stop calling me 'savage.' I mean, by your good graces or whatever. It's insulting, and I'm not even Native American. Plus, I have a name."

"Very well, I will humor you. What would you have me call you?"

"Maria."

"And I bet you're also Católica, right?" I ask through my laughter.

"It's none of your business," she says. "But, yes, I'm Catholic."

"Vale. ¿Cómo no?"

"What's funny?" she says. "Mamí brought us up in the church. I even went to Santa Clara University. That's where I met Carlos—though he was never much of a student."

Savages in the church, I think. Savages in the university. I don't know whether to laugh or cry or slaughter the savage for her insolence. But all I say is, "So the padres have been hard at work."

We cross the Bay Bridge in light traffic, as it's still well before dawn. Our voyage has lasted just over four hours. The savage Maria inexpertly navigates the city, running red lights and driving the wrong direction down one-way streets. Eventually, we arrive in the Financial District, and the savage peers up at the towering buildings, searching for Haege's office, as if she'll recognize it by sight. She seems to be counting in some number system I do not recognize. After more than an hour and a thousand wrong turns, she pulls over and kills the Dakota.

"We're here, Baskets. Now, you can put your sword away."

"But how can I know you're telling the truth? With your cunning savage mind and lying savage tongue?"

She seems to ignore me, staring straight ahead. "Frankly, I don't give a damn one way or the other, but the big gray one with the mermaid fountain's his building. Suite 303."

"Excelente," I say. "My gold at last!"

I stretch my stiff legs toward the curb. I'm about to slam the door when she says, "It's none of my business, but if you really intend on stealing my gold—"

"Correction. My gold."

"—I hope you brought something stronger than your little sword."

"A conquistador is always prepared," I say, grinning. "But now you've piqued my curiosity. Why do you mention it?"

"Ever heard of a safe?"

¡Puta madre! Another obstacle. Still, I indulge in a hearty chuckle to save face. "Thus spake the savage," I say. "Your insight is obvious. I will not dispatch you, however, as your escort has proved most useful. I release you to your fate."

I'm about to say, "Vaya con Díos," but she makes an unexpected gesture with both middle fingers and says, "Good luck with your windmills, Señor." Then she fires up the Dakota and disappears into the maze of dark streets.

THE BUILDING IS OPEN, and the guard at the desk is snoring into his coffee. I march up the stairs to the third floor, then prowl around in the half-light until I find a door marked Haege Numismatic Services. The lock gives me no trouble, but just as I enter, cacophony erupts from speakers mounted near the door.

Though the flashing lights give me vertigo, my instincts and experience take over. I slaughter the speakers, then trace the wires back to their source, into which I plunge my steel. I'm rewarded with a sizzling jolt of defiance, though it's nothing but the enemy's death throes. Then, I slay the lights with equal celerity. I watch and listen. When I'm certain there will be no reinforcements, the search begins.

Oddly, I cannot hear or taste the gold at all, and I can hardly even smell it. All I find in these small, shabby offices is paper— boxes and drawers and binders full of it. Some with images of coins, most with dates, numbers, and indecipherable descriptions. I become frustrated and hack up more than one piece of hostile furniture, but just as discovery begets violence, violence also begets discovery. There, beneath the splintering detritus of one of the slaughtered desks, I find what I'm looking for. Almost. It's the nefarious safe to which the savage alluded.

The warm scent of gold—my gold—wafts from deep within its locked chamber.

I have a plan, and I follow it, but the strong box proves to be a worthy adversary. It refuses to yield to my steel, fighting it off almost without trying. I swipe and hack, stab and chop, all to no avail. Though I'm robust and hale, stronger than a team of oxen and with greater endurance, I know when I've been bested. Drenched in sweat, panting for breath, I sink to the floor.

I must devise a new plan.

Perhaps, I nod off from exhaustion. I cannot be certain. I'm still recovering when Haege blunders in.

I'm on my feet, sword brandished, before he rounds the corner.

He eyes me for a moment. Then, coward that he is, turns to flee. I block his path with my blade. His face blanches, and I expect him to faint. His veins do not flow with *conquistador* blood.

"Okay, okay," he practically sobs.

I aim my chin at the safe. "Open it."

"Not the Paradise Mountain hoard."

"Claro que sí."

"I can't."

"You shall."

"I won't."

I sigh and mutter under my breath. Why must they all make my job so tiresome?

"Should you refuse to comply, I will first cut off your ears and stuff them into your mouth. Then, your nose will follow. I will then slice off your fingers, one by one, followed by your hands at the wrist, then your arms at the elbow. Your toes will follow, then your feet at the ankles, then your legs at the knee. And on and on, a slow, grueling juggernaut of pain, until you open the box. Or, when you're no longer able, until you spit out your ears and nose and tell me how to open it." I flash my most menacing grin. "Though I think you will not give up more than a finger or two. ¿No?"

Haege looks as if he may vomit. Then, in an acrid cloud of fear-stench, he drops to his knees and begins manipulating a black dial. He enters a magical sequence of numbers, twists a handle, and the intractable safe opens like the legs of a loose savage.

I expect to be blinded by the radiance of El Dorado in miniature; yet apparently, Haege stores all his coins in sacks, so the luster is not visible. Even so, I'm overwhelmed by the taste and smell. I remove the heavy sacks, unzip one to verify their contents—¡oro mio!—then pile them into duffle bags Haege supplies. The gold fills two of them—quite a haul—but it's heavy, so at my polite request, Haege helps me downstairs with the bags. We locate his Cherokee and load the bags into the back.

I take his keys, then say, "I am borrowing your Indian with your permission. ¿Verdad?"

He shakes his head once, biting his lip, then perceives my scowl and nods vigorously.

"Please, Señor, use your tongue."

"Yes," he says. "It's yours. Keep it as long as you like."

"Muy amable," I say, "muy generoso."

He gazes back dumbly. I should strike him dead with a swipe of my blade, then burn his office to the ground. Instead, I beam at him as I open the Indian's door, leaving him to revel in ignorance and ignominy.

A fate worse than death.

I FIND MY WAY TO La Misión de Nuestra Padre San Francisco de Asís. It would be easy to locate, even without my superior navigational skills, since there are signs all over the city guiding me there, as if toward my destiny. I speak briefly to the *jefe*, Padre Juan Dólar, who permits me to take refuge deep within the church cloisters. Yet he is no fool. He asks that I make an offering in return for shelter, either daily or in one lump sum. The choice is mine. He knows that I know that he knows I could as easily massacre the entire lot of them as breathe—and I mean everyone. Priests, altar boys, choir, parishioners, even the mendicants supping in the courtyard. Of course, I'd never do it. Not in the *casa de Díos*. Perhaps, not anywhere. I opt for a daily contribution, which I present at midday Mass.

Everyone is content, at least for a while. I follow the *padre's* counsel and keep to my chambers. I spend my time studying the history of the mythical place that I, along with the priests and my brothers-in-arms, helped to usher into being, the paradise of Calafia made fact by blood, sweat, and prayers.

Yet I grow bored and restless, especially since so much ink is devoted to the savages. Such capitulation tarnishes the glory of our heroic exploits. It's shameful. Still, I take comfort in my own superlative conquest. I have more gold now than I could spend, if spending it were ever the point, for with gold comes power. I've been on the losing end of a glorious history for far too long. From now on, the world shall bend to my will.

When I do emerge from my seclusion, it's either to dine or attend Mass. Except at Holy Communion, no one speaks to me, other than to coax me to make a full confession of my sins. I'll admit it's been a while, perhaps more than a century, but I'm in no mood for Hail Marys. Anyway, the others at the mission remain aloof, curious but intimidated. I act erratically, tossing bowls of food onto the floor and shredding tapestries with my sword, just to keep them on edge.

I spend one or two nights a week prowling for wenches. It was bound to happen, though I try to be as discreet as possible so as not to put my hosts in an awkward position.

I quickly learn that my gold has changed everything. Its luster makes for easy conquests—too easy. I don't even have to try. It's not long before I grow nostalgic for the long, lean years, when pinning down a shrieking savage was the only gratification possible.

Time passes in a slow blur.

Then one morning, a month or so after my arrival, Padre Dólar raps at my chamber door.

"Señor Vásquez? You have visitors."

"Is it the King's ambassadorial dispatch?"

"I'm afraid not," he says, worrying the crucifix around his neck.

"They strike me as backwoods ruffians."

"I know no one who fits this description."

"Nevertheless, they seem to know you. We've turned them away twice before, but this time, they seem more insistent. Perhaps, you could send them on their way in person? More forcefully? I've had the vicar and deacon lay drop cloths in the nave."

I nod, though I have no taste for slaughter.

I smell them before I see them, a cloud of unwashed funk. Three grizzled mountain men with long beards and tattered clothes.

I've never laid eyes on them before, but I know at once why they are here. They've come for the gold.

"There he is."

"Fella we been looking for."

"Man o' the hour."

"I have come at your request," I say. "What business have you here?"

They chuckle, chew their tobacco, and spit on the pews, hymnals, and floors. They don't have six teeth among them.

"The gold, fancy-pants."

"We dug it up to begin with, so it belongs to us."

"Now, hand it over."

The pickaxes and shovels they brandish are nothing. I unsheathe my sword in the murky afternoon light filtering through the stained glass.

"Be gone, or I shall flay you with my steel."

"Stand your ground, boys."

"He ain't gonna do nothing in a church."

"It's all just for show."

Although it's not what I want to do, they have left me no choice.

"Be gone at once, or these floors shall run red with your blood."

Now, they're on their feet, wafting their stench around, likely curling the pages of the missals.

"Keep calm, boys."

"He ain't gonna disgrace his Pope.

"Nor ruin all them saintly relics."

In three quick strokes, I slice them each on the left cheek. These are only flesh wounds, though deep enough to draw blood and eventually to scar, but they have the intended effect. The filthy provincials clutch their wounds and back toward the entrance.

"You ain't seed the last of us, prissy pants."

"We'll be back."

"We want that gold!"

I sheathe my sword, then shoulder the door shut, barring it behind me.

NOT A FULL DAY PASSES before another group of men I've never seen pays me an unannounced visit.

I've just laid down for my *siesta* when I hear shouting and heavy footsteps downstairs. Soon they're at my door. They, too, stink—the odor sharp and musty, sour with sweat and blood, rum and brine.

"Avast ye, landlubber," shouts a man with yellow teeth and eyes, gnawing on a wet cigar stump. He may be inebriated. It's possible they all are. "We've come for your pieces of eight."

"Keep your voice down please," I say, sitting up. "This is a house of worship."

"Doubloons, scurvy dog." The other men chortle and howl.

"Or would ye rather we rape, pillage, and plunder on your hallowed ground?"

By now I'm standing. "What's mine is mine. There is nothing for you here."

The yellow-eyed captain catches me unawares, pressing his rusty cutlass to my throat. "We won't ask twice, scallywag. Now take us to the loot!"

"Está bien," I say. "But my Cherokee has it."

"Injun, you say?" He gnaws on his cigar stump. "Then lead the way, wastrel."

The pirates follow me into the blinding afternoon sunshine. I stop at the Cherokee and nonchalantly paw the keys.

The captain swills from a bottle of rum, wipes his mouth on the back of his filthy sleeve, then asks, "So, where be your Injun?"

"Very near," I say. I slide in behind the wheel, then slam and lock the door. I crank the engine and crack the window. "I'll meet you at Fisherman's Wharf. Have some drinks and wait for me. I'll be back, pronto."

Then, I disappear with the gold.

My gold.

I'M BACK TO THE MISSION in time for dinner. I sense that my continued presence has begun to cause some consternation among the *padres*. I do not wish to be a burden, so I explain my intentions to Padre Dólar and arrange for an introduction at La Misión del Gloriosisimo Patriarca San Jose. He tries to dissuade me from leaving, promising increased security and protection, but his empty words cannot sway me.

It's still well before dawn when I make my exit. At this hour the roads are empty all the way down to San Jose.

When I arrive, I'm unable to locate the mission. I know it should be at the heart of the *pueblo*, but try as I might, I cannot find it. I stop to refill the Cherokee, and I ask directions from the savage behind the counter.

She studies me with her suspicious savage eyes, then says, "Wrong city, amigo. That's up in Fremont."

"Savage," I say, "you make no sense."

"Ten-fifteen miles north," she says. "Anything else?"

I turn and pull open the door.

"That's $63.81 for the gas."

I withdraw a gold coin from the pocket of my breeches and flip it to her. Her eyes go wide as she traces its arc, though I'm gone before she catches it.

I drive around in circles for a while longer, but the mission is nowhere to be found. Perhaps this is another example of savage cunning? I soon remember that there's another in Santa Clara, so I follow the signs and take the marked exit. I know it's located off El Camino Real, or The King's Highway, but it takes a while to find, for it's hidden in an endless sea of identical domiciles and places of business. As I eventually discover, La Misión Santa Clara is on a university campus. There are students everywhere, though they look neither pious nor scholarly, grinning, laughing, playing games with balls and disks.

They ignore me. I ignore them. I barge through the church doors and make my presence known.

"It is our pleasure to have you here, Señor Vásquez," says Padre Marinara. "Shall I show you around? Or would you prefer to rest after your journey?"

I mull over the offer for a moment, squinting through the stained glass toward the parking lot. "Will my Cherokee be safe?"

"Your—?"

His question hangs in the musty air. I say nothing, waiting.

"Yes, of course, it will be fine." He seems nonplussed. "You have nothing to fear."

"Excelente," I say, stepping away from the window and pretending to examine the altarpiece. "Please, show me your mission's splendors."

The *padre* must have little to do because he gives me a long tour, providing such excruciating detail that it takes us an hour to leave the chapel. He peppers his comments with offhand questions of a prying, personal nature. He also mentions a recent gold heist that is even now circulating in the newspapers. As he shows me my chambers in the Jesuit residence, he hands me the Mass schedule and encourages me to fill the mission coffers with as much as I might manage.

"So that we may continue to bring God's light to those in greatest need," he says.

"Yes, of course," I say. "Now, you must tell me. There is space for my Indian here?"

Again, he seems baffled. "Yes, there's an underground parking garage. I'll see that you get a pass."

His words bring much relief. After all, until I move the gold, I can't be too careful.

My FIRST FEW WEEKS at Mission Santa Clara pass quietly. I keep to my quarters, reading more histories about our glorious conquests. The food is good and plentiful, too, and none of the other brethren ask any personal questions.

On one of my first moonlit walks, I discover that wine and wenches are in no short supply. They may be university students and children of God, but their jokes are bawdy and their innuendo salacious. I see no reason why I should not seek my gratification with them.

One night, upon my return from wenching, I'm startled to discover a visitor waiting for me in my chambers. A savage.

He's lying on my bed and leafing through an old issue of *America* magazine.

I unsheathe my sword, point it at his chin, and say, "Leave at once, or you shall meet your Maker."

"Know what, ese?" he says, daring to speak. "Not much of what they say in here's really true."

"You test my patience, savage."

He sits up and drops the magazine on the nightstand. "Been out boozing, huh? I miss a good draft Dos Equis every once in a while."

My rage begins to boil. This savage has no respect. I grind my teeth and growl, "Get out immediately, or I shall lop off your head and pitch it out the window."

"Tranquilo, bro." He makes no effort to dissemble his mirth. "Ain't worth all that effort. Sounds messy, too."

I exaggerate, adjusting my grip on the hilt of my steel. "I will not tell you again. Depart this instant, or suffer my wrath."

"No way, homes. You gotta tell me about all them ladies you been getting." He chuckles. "Plus, we got something serious to discuss."

This savage galls me like no other. Why, I know not.

"Ain't no other way to put it," he says. "You took something belongs to my missus."

I can tolerate his insolence no longer. Without considering the repercussions, I close my eyes and swing my sword at the savage's neck with all my might. My blade is sharp; it should only take one blow. Except, I meet no resistance.

"Nice try, vato, but no dice." He smiles to himself and wags his savage head. "Listen, you want me to go, I'll go. But we ain't finished, right? You and me got business."

Then he's gone.

I'M STROLLING BACK FROM MIDDAY MASS when the savage appears from the breezeway of one of the university buildings. It's been less than a week, and I can't say I'm pleased to see him. After all, he can only be after one thing. Gold. My gold. At first, he doesn't say anything, just walks a short distance with me, but it doesn't last.

"So, you got Maria's gold."

I'm unaccustomed to his blunt way of speaking, but I decide to humor him.

"Never heard of her."

"Man, don't act all dumb." Somehow he leads me over to a bench in a quiet, secluded garden. "Unless you recently stole a shitload of gold from somebody else?"

"Anything is possible," I say, staring off into the distance.

The savage looks frustrated. "Let me be real clear, Baskets. You went up to the cabin and took what belongs to Maria."

"Where, apparently, I'd misplaced it."

The savage stares at me with his savage eyes. "You serious, bro? That don't even make sense."

Two long-legged wenches saunter through the garden. They are sumptuous, though they stare at me as if I'm insane or worse.

"Little young for you, no?"

I brandish my blade and shout, "Silence, savage!"

"That sword stuff don't work, remember?" He smiles his savage smile. "And, by the way, my name ain't Savage."

I play along. "Then, what do you call yourself?"

"Carlos."

"Very well," I say, imagining the catharsis I'll feel when I finally plunge my blade into his belly.

All at once, hoards of students swarm around the campus, laughing, discoursing, fiddling with glowing rectangular cellular phones.

"Ain't no other way to say it, bro. The gold you took don't belong to you. Now, you got to give it back, right?"

"Incorrect," I say.

He shakes his head. "You're off your nut, homes. Anyway, what are you gonna do with it? So far, it ain't brought you nothing but trouble."

I turn my sword in my hand, watching the sunlight play across the blade's sharp edges. I regret to admit that he's right. I've had no end of grief since I laid my hands on that gold. Except with the wenches, of course.

"I defy you or anyone else to force my hand," I say.

Then, without warning or hesitation, I flip my steel over and plunge it into his gut. I feel a surge of satisfaction, until I realize I've somehow missed. The savage stands behind the bench, chuckling. It takes all my manly strength to dislodge the blade.

"Hardheaded, no?" he says. "I'll ask you once more nicely. Will you return the gold to Maria?"

"That's entirely out of the question."

"Come on, man. She needs it more than you do. Trust me. She's got back taxes on the cabin, and the insurance wasn't enough. Her *abuelo* built that place with his own hands. She could lose it and the land, Baskets." He studies my reaction. "Our house ain't but a couple blocks away. I'll even walk you over."

"I shall not be moved." I stand and stretch my legs, then sheathe my sword. "Now, this conversation is over."

"We'll see about that, Baskets."

ALL IS WELL FOR A WEEK, maybe two. I spend my days in my chambers reading and thinking, and I even begin writing my memoirs, *The True and Complete History of Juan Francisco Hernán Vásquez de Léon,*

Conquistador. To the victor go the spoils; also, the power of history. I sup with the brethren and attend Mass, daily. Everyone seems content with my presence at Mission Santa Clara.

Everyone but Padre Marinara. I've successfully avoided him since I first arrived.

All at once, something changes, and he refuses to leave me in peace. He catches me with my chamber door unlocked and barges in while I'm working on my memoirs.

"Good afternoon, Señor Vásquez. Peace be with you."

"And also with you, Padre." I force myself to be courteous, even deferential. "How might I be of service to you, Señor?"

"Forgive me for troubling you with such a trifling matter, but since your arrival, we have noticed a sharp influx of gold coins in the daily offering."

Avarice is everywhere. I say, "I understand, Padre. I appreciate the generosity with which you have welcomed me to your parish. If it were possible to double the contribution, would that be satisfactory?"

He leans against the desk, his face glowing eerily, and makes a holy chapel of his fingers. "I'm not sure, Vásquez. There is so much need in our community, and our funds are limited."

He smiles and waits.

I say nothing.

It takes only a few seconds for an annoyed pucker to overtake his face. "The coins we've received were minted in the mid-to-late-1800's, most of them in San Francisco. We've seen nothing but five dollar coins, though they'll generate far more than their face value." Again, he waits, a sticky smile emerging from his pucker.

"Then, you'd prefer higher denominations?"

"That's not exactly what I'm getting at, Vásquez." He shifts his weight. "What can you tell me about the Paradise Mountain gold hoard, recently reported stolen?"

"Certainly, less than you already know, Padre."

He dons a pleasant mask, opens the door, and scans the hallway. Then, he closes the door and locks it.

"Let me spell it out for you, Spaniard. Half."

"Half?"

"That's right. You want to stay here in peace and tranquility? Then I get half the gold."

"With all due respect, Señor, your terms are unacceptable."

Hand on my hilt, I prepare to face him in battle, which means hacking him to death in a bloody frenzy, if I can manage. My threatening posture must seem convincing, because he says, "Don't be so hasty, Vásquez."

I lean against the bed.

He gloats. "Tomorrow, after Mass. Either you share the wealth, or—

"Yes, please tell me. Or what?"

"Difficult to say," he says, swallowing a chuckle. "Just know this. It will be out of my hands."

AFTER THE PADRE LEAVES, I take a long walk, cursing the *hijo de puta* in the most florid, colorful way. I catch myriad suspicious glances from savages, but I need not take my sword from its scabbard to send them scurrying.

Once night falls, I slake my thirst at a *cantina* near the mission where wenches are known to cavort. It's a necessary distraction. The music's at high volume, the rhythm throbbing in my chest. A well-placed gold coin keeps my cup full all night. I return to the bar for a breather from nonstop dancing and guzzle my wine, which increasingly tastes like *aguardiente*.

"Having fun, Baskets?"

I glance over. The savage!

"Happy to see me, right?"

"Why must you refuse to obey my explicit command?"

He ignores me. He's the most impudent savage I've ever encountered. The bartender pours him a *cerveza* he doesn't touch.

"The padre came to see you today, no?"

"And how would you—?"

He exaggerates a wink. "Now, you feel me, homes?"

A sour taste invades my mouth. I slug Carlos' beer and order another. "Marinara gets nothing," I say, panting. "It has taken me almost five-hundred years to acquire my gold. I will relinquish what is rightfully mine to no man."

"That's good, cuz it don't belong to no man."

Without warning, the beer that's in front of me splashes over my head. I scan to my left and right, swivel to see behind me. The bartender's at the far end of the room pouring Goldschlager for a gaggle of inebriated wenches. No one's paying us the least bit of attention. No one but the grinning savage.

"Plus," he says, "ain't nothing you stole 'rightfully' yours."

"Gracias para la explicación," I say, sliding off my stool. "Now if you'll excuse me, the wenches are calling."

I take no more than two steps before I'm sprawling face-down on the insalubrious floor. I scramble to my feet and shout, "¡Ya basta! You will kindly remove yourself from the premises, or I will slaughter your entire family."

Everyone stares, and the music stops, but the savage is nowhere to be found. I'm screaming threats at an empty barstool.

It takes me ten minutes and too much gold to work my way back into the wenches' good graces. Soon, we're writhing to the rhythm. There shall be ample gratification tonight. Only leave it to the savage to ruin the moment. He sidles up and says, "Who was you yelling at, bro?"

"Would that you had vanished for good."

He laughs. "So, you changed your mind yet?"

Our verbal sparring seems to have attracted the wenches' attention. Perhaps a good tongue lashing will titillate them further. "You have two minutes to disappear," I shout over the thumping music, unsheathing my sword. "If you remain in the vicinity, I shall thrust my blade into your heart."

"Is that a fact?" says the savage.

I feel his eyes boring through me. The wenches, too, seem to be staring. The room feels suddenly drafty.

"Hey, Baskets, what happened to your shirt?"

I glance down. It hangs in tatters, the sleeves and body shredded.

"You shall suffer for this impudence." I swing my sword back for a mighty blow but almost impale myself upon the blade, as I stumble to the floor. When I try to stand, I realize that my ankles are roped together with my belt.

The wenches point and laugh.

I cast the belt aside and prepare to slaughter Carlos. I'm certain I will relish his every scream as I slowly butcher him.

Before I can hack off his arms or lop off his legs, the music stops, and everyone's eyes are on me. For a moment, there's not a sound. Then, all at once, the savages explode, some falling out of their chairs in hysterics. I wonder what has tickled them so, and then I realize my breeches are down around my ankles. I'm stark naked in the middle of the room. Worst of all, my manhood has pruned and shriveled, from the room's chill, from the monumental embarrassment.

Mercifully, the young wenches say nothing I can hear, though their disapproving gazes follow me as I shrink toward the door, swordless and beltless, clutching a fistful of breeches in each hand. The ignominy.

BACK IN MY CHAMBERS, I slink into bed and weep silently into my pillow. In all my years, never once have I suffered such humiliation. Why has nothing good come of the gold?

I haven't been in bed fifteen minutes when I see the savage hovering over me.

"Hey, Baskets? You awake?"

He clicks on the night table lamp.

"Please," I beg, covering my eyes, "leave me in peace."

"Then, you're finally ready to play ball?"

"Anything," I hear myself say, "to make the indignities stop."

"Seriously?" He chuckles. "Like you'll paint my house? And wax my Impala? Maybe wait in line for me at the DMV?"

His words are all savage gibberish. "Yes, yes, anything," I moan.

"Naw, bro, I'm just yanking your chain." He grabs the desk chair and slides it over next to the bed. "But you see the kind of perks that come with my condition, right?"

"Yes, yes, your powers are worthy of awe. Now, please, tell me what I must do to be rid of you once and for all."

"That's easy, ese. All you gotta do is give back the gold."

"Take it," I say. "It's in the closet behind you."

He investigates, unzipping one of the duffles and admiring a handful of glimmering coins.

"No shit, man? It was here the whole time?"

"Now, will you please just leave?"

In the amber glow of the lamp, the savage looks pensive. After a long moment, he says, "Sorry, bro. Can't do that. You gotta return it yourself."

"Be that as it may, I have no energy for another journey into the distant sierra."

"Sierra? No, Baskets, like I told you, our house is just around the corner, maybe two blocks from here. The cabin's just for weekends."

He waits. I wait. Dawn leaks in through the window.

"Come on, man. Get up," he says. "I'll show you the way."

THE DOMICILE OF WHICH THE SAVAGE SPEAKS is further than he lets on, though at this point, I'd carry the gold back to Spain to be rid of it.

We arrive at a stucco bungalow, the small front garden filled with bright bougainvillea and an array of succulents. I bang on the front door and wait. No response. Next door, a hound begins to bay. I bang some more. Nothing. I turn to the savage, but he has disappeared again.

"Go away!" she yells through the door.

"It is I, Señora."

"Don't know anyone by that name. And I've got a gun."

"Juan Francisco Hernán Vásquez de Léon."

"Baskets?"

"If you must."

"Why'd you come here? To steal my truck?"

"Only to return what belongs to you."

She opens the door but not the screen. "Have you been drinking, Baskets?"

"Sí," I say, "but that's not the point." I drop the bags at her feet. "Here is your gold. Please forgive any torment its absence has caused you."

The *señora* opens the screen and waves me inside. I drag the gold into the kitchen. She pours coffee, and we sit at the table together.

"That's a kind gesture, Baskets. Kind of strange, too. But you can take it with you when you go. I don't want it."

Since unearthing the gold, the *señora* explains, she's had no end of dubious visitors, from a group of middle-aged men with metal detectors, to several different bands of bank robbers, to all manner of crooks, thieves, and con artists. Also, me.

"Even after you took it, the greedy creeps just kept on coming. Last week, it was forty-niners. Yesterday, it was pirates. I don't want to know what tomorrow might bring."

The *señora* brews another pot of coffee. We sit in comfortable silence. She makes no mention of my previous threats of violence, which I'm surprised to realize bring me bottomless shame. I'm actually pleased to have left my sword behind at the *cantina*. All the same, I know that, even as we sit here sipping coffee, malefactors and villains of every stripe are coming for the gold. The *señora*, too, must recognize this fact.

"I've got a proposition for you," she says.

"Yes?"

"First, do you really not want that gold? Free and clear, a gift from me to you?"

I consider her offer for a moment. Without conquest, there can be no glory.

"I would not take it if my life depended on it."

"Then grab the loot," she says, "and follow me."

The *señora* leads me across the back garden to a small shed among palms, cedars, and cypress. She grabs a pair of shovels, hands me one, and grins.

"Let's put this gold back into the ground."

The *señora* locates a spot off the back corner of her deck. We dig for what feels like hours but may be only ten or fifteen minutes. When we've fashioned a sizable hole, we drop in the bags and tamp down the dirt. Then, we drag over a huge *terracotta* pot full of tulips and position it over the hole.

"Thanks, Baskets. I owe you one."

"You owe me nothing," I say and mean it. I feel a warmth blooming in my chest. "And please forgive me for threatening your life."

"Never mind," she says. "That's all forgotten."

We put the shovels away, and I prepare to take my leave. Although I'm uncertain how to broach the subject, I say, "We now have a mutual acquaintance."

"Who's that?"

"Carlos."

"My Carlos?" she says, almost glowing.

"He's the one who led me to your house." I expect to end there but cannot help myself. "He convinced me to return the gold to you."

"That's just like him." We pause at the side gate. "I hope he wasn't too rough on you."

I feel an honest grin overtake my physiognomy. "I can report that he's in fine form."

The *señora* chuckles. "No wonder you seem so subdued."

We listen to the breeze play through the palm fronds. Hummingbirds thrum and whistle around the bougainvillea.

"The time has come for me to say *adieu*, Señora."

"Where will you go?" she asks. "What will you do?"

I take a deep breath. I have not yet considered the matter. "I must trust in God," I say, "and follow my fate."

She seems to mull over my words over for a time. "More of us should have such faith," she says.

I turn and make for the sidewalk. For the first time I can remember, I have no destination, no scheme, nothing to guide my quest.

"Hey, Baskets?" Maria calls behind me. "Think fast!"

I turn in time to see her flip something into the air. A coin, glittering and golden in the morning sunlight. I trace its slow arc and catch it in my right hand.

"There's more gold?"

"You missed the other safe."

I turn the coin in my hand, watching the play of sunlight over its surface.

"It's a $20 Double Eagle," she says. "Could be worth a million dollars!"

"I cannot accept this, Señora."

"It's yours, Baskets. You earned it." She smiles warmly. "Plus, I've got a half-dozen more just like it. I'm selling them on eBay. You should probably do the same."

"Very well. I thank you most humbly. Now, as I take my leave, allow me to declare that—"

"The shortest goodbyes are the best, Baskets."

I swallow, confused for a moment. "In that case, Señora, I bid you a fond farewell."

"Same to you," she says.

"Buena suerte, Maria."

She smiles warmly. "Vaya con Díos, Baskets."

As I wander down the sidewalk, birds atwitter on the power lines, my heart feels light, my mind clear. After so much questing, I have found what I never knew I was seeking.

At last, I'm free.

Noel Conneely

TOBY WALDRON

Toby Waldron loved.
His love was soft with no centre.
He loved Marlyn Munroe. How she walked.
How she wore her stockings black.
If she had a yen for math
he might have gone to her to ask
how to add the two and two of love
to the one and one of only.
She could teach him innocence.
She could teach him wonder.
And all through the fair he searched
for girls like Marlyn with no luck.
And on the swinging boats
he pulled the rope to climb above
the muddle of his days.
He thought of her in the seat across
holding her frock and her breath
each time the boat came down,
her nails digging into the soft wood.
But soon, he would get off and hear again
the raucous call of ticket sellers,
the cries of luckless gamblers.
He would lose himself in the crowd.
He didn't want people he knew
finding him alone with no one,
for Melody Malone put out the story

that when she kissed him
the kiss was so bad
she had to wipe her mouth on her sleeve.
His heart was being pulled apart
and the sun was going down pink
and he wished he were in a field
of buttercups fluttering in the wind
where the dear old what-me nots sing
and a word doesn't have to be a word
but notes of a half or a third and the bells
ring the ding all day.

John J. Trause

HYDRATION, HYDRATION, HYDRATION

Wozu Dichter in dürftiger Zeit? What are poets for in a destitute time?
                                    —Johann Holderlin

Folks these days are so concerned
about the state of their hydration
that they carry around water bottles wherever they go.
Why is it that this infantilization,
this drive for the bottle
transcends the usual etiquette of time and place?

A baby whines in the sanctuary.
A toddler tips the table.

Personal hydration as a public good,
a basic human right,
is played out before the powers that be.
The greatest good has come to be the right to choose
to regulate the state of one's hydration.

You will see them everywhere:
Bottles in the schools, at the library
where drink is prohibited, in the supermarket,
on the bus. Bottles at the latest lecture,
at town hall and the post office. Bottles
on the train, at a church service,
and the meeting of the PTA—Oh, I mean PTO.

Bottles at the theater. Bottles
in the park, at the party, and at the picnic.
Bottles on the beaches, bottles on the tarmac,
bottles in the fields, and in the streets.
Bottles in the hills. Surrender.

When systems fail, when sub-and-super-structure
crumble, when the pyramid is leveled,
the bottle stands,
and the bottle will be the ruin of us all.

Cheryl J. Fish

FLEXIBLE BARK

after evacuation
after afternoon
where are we?
who are they?

some could not run
some fell from buildings
some made it into boats

the wrong ones said go home

do images disappear?
who recalls landfill from before towers,
sand dunes where artists performed?
who builds buildings, and who demolishes them?
who are the artful and who lack vision?

who desires revenge?
who follows orders?

the Lenape built dwellings of flexible bark
on this island
before it bore the weight of iron and steel

smoke escaped from cooking fires
in their
dome roofs covered with bark

who thinks of them?

what does it say
if nobody does?

who sings
when we run?

Cheryl J. Fish

ALL THE ASH

All the ash of my life smudges the margins of this page
　　　Ashes fleck my radio mind

with surprises of great and fallow tunes
It is that or this? A sullen peak of boo?
　　　The comic, the classic, the getaway
near and yet just missing a mark

Ash of dark dreams with bright white lines
Does that mean you can always escape?
Might you
toss and turn into the respectable every day?

Ash on my forehead, ash in my shirt
Am I a token table statistic, or burned partial tree?
Nearly grown and realized, then stopped
　　　By fact, force, or infiltration?

By the seat of the sea
By the ribbon of the climate
By the relief of those escaped,
of those that want to go backwards, break us down
build and build and build 'til there's no light in the city sky
With ash we paint a redolent world

It enters our bodies

Rebecca Lilly

HAIKU

i.
Falls froth on the rocks—
In pools below, clouds mirror
through cedar and fir tops

ii.
Spontaneous and
effortless, how thought should be:
Here, then dissolving—

iii.
The noises of rain
and wind receding through pines...
lengthening silence

iv.
Shadows of bare oaks
knocked by the gusts; through branches:
sunlight on rock dust

v.
In the gulf between
existing things, potential:
Invisible being...

vi.
Fir needles. The crow
peers through, his beak visible;
disappearing moon…

vii.
The seer said, "From life
to life, our dream runs, as we
laugh, cry, disappear…"

Simon Perchik

C76

This pebble is still thirsty
and though it no longer speaks
must know it will be brought back

as a lake and on the surface
a night where there was none before.
You are always listening for black—

a coat, the shadow. A mourner lets go
as if there's no other way to drink
except from a hand left open

lifting this hillside to your lips
where underground streams return
as fingertips, salt, and silence.

Craig Evenson

RECOMPENSE

As we shared
our disappointment
in the movie

a deer appeared
in the headlights.

Not the hypnotized idiom
but fully functional,

unable to imagine
the ways things die,

not transfixed
the way I was

by the stilled, strobed,
deer-shaped cavity,

how its gravity
crushed the day,

eying life
on the other side.

Craig Evenson

BENCH

I loaded it into the back of the truck
from the end of a driveway
because it was free

set it in the yard,
a seat for the sun

for the leaves'
sharp shadows

the hidden whip
of the cardinal

the parasitic silence
inside the trees

and, from the brush pile,
the rasp of the wren
spending its penny lungs

the Delphic lichen
rivaling the spaces
between the leaves
in its shades
from gray to green:

marks that things made
will degrade
into meaning

hearable
as when my dying
wakes early
to talk a little;
and because it's not talking to me
and I get to forget each word,
I listen and
hear my part,
expendable element
whose absence claps
into a fresh perfection

Joseph Bottone

GOING OVER

i.

I would be a tree for your shade.

And if you came to me with language I could
decipher, what code would you use,

as when angels speak?
The quick-footed Hermes—
Is he still in your employ?

And if I am moved to distraction,
what cost to me.
What loss. And if I were not,

Paradise would burn brighter.
I'd be empty of all
but your attributes.

Holding dialogue with myself.
Yes, I say. Yes.

And if my kisses were your feet, and
your feet my eyes,

I'd run to where the light is brightest and
shatter into ten thousand gems.

ii.

I crawl into sleep
        imagining the Emerald City
living in my head

When the moon settles
        in dawn's ocean
I awake bewildered,
unaccustomed again to this world.

We sing our songs; the songbirds sing:
        "I heard a minstrel chant.
They sang me my heart's desire.
        I sang what they sang.
I was where they were,
        and they were where I am"[1]

I see light, see myself.
        A vague form
startles me

        —in this strange land, the trees, the wind
and the singers of songs know better
conspiring for the transfiguration of the earth.

[1]Fakhruddin 'Iraqi

Joseph Bottone

SITTING

Sometimes a tiger prowls the room
         keeping its eye out for anything
    that moves.
A hunger gnaws
deep in its bones.

    Its paws resonate. With each step
a miasma of dust like a stain glows
where it prowls,
intent on grasping.

And when the tiger-mind
settles down,
    a cooing dove.

    Touch it, light streams.

Everywhere.

Matthew T. Hummer

ANY OF US

A DISTANT HUM AS WE HIKED into the woods. The growing echo of cicada drowned out the car noise. Mathias, my son, told me the ridged layers that jutted out of the leaf mat were sedimentary stones. They had pressed together underground, but not so long ago as to become metamorphic. I told him he should be a scientist. He trusts the way the forest proves textbook words.

He said all the bugs in the world outweigh all the humans, because of all the bugs that lived underground. I asked what they were hiding from.

I thought about how I had once dug dirt from the garden to fill a pot for a plant and pressed loam between the root ball and the plastic wall of the container. I sat on the stoop and let the sun warm my skin. A roly poly and an inchworm rose through the surface of the earth. The segmented green worm horseshoed himself across, and the roly poly dug. A clump of dirt moved up and down while he burrowed. Then, the surface stopped moving.

Charlie Roberts killed the Amish girls in Nickel Mines. That day I drove past the area on my way to West Chester. Route 30 East, north of the shooting. Helicopters buzzed like gnats.

The Wawa lot was full of news vans. Turkey vultures. The black hovering wings that circled me, napping in the summer grass as a boy. The inner flesh deepened to burgundy when a cloud screened the sun.

I could have approached one of these vans and said, "I knew Charlie Roberts." Floodlight and microphone. But what would I say? That I knew him as a boy. That I tried not to make fun of him in the school's brick hallway. That he peed himself on the hiking trail in the Adirondacks. That once, riding the back of my father's trash truck working from dumpster-to-dumpster in the apartment complex near the mall—when the wind lashed and steel handles bit through cotton—I remembered the boy and reached out to God for him. I was fifteen. That was decades before the milk truck, lubricant, tape, and guns.

Mathias and I hiked up switchbacks to the Horseshoe Trail. The hum of cars sounded like a mosquito swarm. The mud trail led to a stone logging road. A sign said this was a joint project of Middle Creek and a logging company. Logging machines sat in a tangle of trees. Sinews of inner bark twisted open like Japanese lanterns, splattered with red dirt. One yellow machine had O-link chains on its massive tires, tires that had turned the hilltop meadow to a coursing river of mud. The path narrowed in the distance like a snake's tail, a pile of harvested trunks piled to the side.

We traveled down a muddy path on the eastern slope. We were looking for the ruined homestead. Along that trail there was an old beech tree with initials scarred into it. The vow of lovers.

In 1986, Charlie's uncle organized a hiking trip to the Adirondacks. I hadn't seen Charlie for a year. He had been attending our grade school, but his parents withdrew him. Andrew, my friend and Charlie's cousin, said that they were "born again." Now, his parents wanted him home-schooled.

To pass time hiking, we boys whittled walking sticks. Our bright points stabbed the leaf mat. Once in a while, a boy-hunter would loft an amphibian into the air at the end of the stick for us to admire— squiggling frogs and toads, stuck.

I wanted to but didn't. I loved animals, and my father was there. He said it was sick. Killing's not a game. "Don't point that gun at me," he would say, when I turned my Lone Ranger silver revolver toward him. He said Vietnam would have been a great place to vacation, if not for the bullets, booby traps, black pajama men, *punji* stakes, malaria, and snakes. He'd sit out at night and smoke and watch the explosions that lit the sky like the Fourth of July.

I don't know for sure if Charlie speared frogs, but in my memory, he held a splayed frog aloft, as if he were a dumb warrior who had joined the vicious tribe of adolescent boys.

Charlie was slow. He talked like boots picking their way across wet rocks in a shallow stream. He laughed like a slow-building earthquake. By the time he reached seventh grade hike, he was afraid to change clothes in front of the other boys. For the hike, he wore his tan t-shirt and camouflaged shorts the whole time.

Charlie was carrying the green bag Mr. Sydorko, a phlegmatic New Jerseyite, had brought. A bag of sugarless doughnuts that were worse than a *fasnacht*. I tried one on the trip and nearly choked on the dry dough.

Lancaster is a land of Shoofly Pie. I grew up thinking Angel Food Cake was a healthy dessert because it was light and had pockets of air.

We were starting off from the cabin, in line on the trail. From the back, Mr. Sydorko yelled, "Hold up."

Charlie stood on the rise of the hump. Mr. Sydorko was next to him. Charlie held the bagel bag out in his right hand, away from his body; his left hand stretched toward the trees. He began to cry like a hurt animal, howling from his slow mouth as a dark spot at his crotch spread.

No one made fun of him. The adults ushered him away to the side of the cabin.

The Horseshoe Trail again, here with Mathias. Centuries echoed in piled stone and round imprints, where log ends once stuck into mortar, a six-inch handmade iron nail bent from a log hole like a broken dog tail. The name "Wentzel" was scratched into mortar from a time before miners or loggers, before the state reclaimed the hills and lake for egret, heron, eagle, Canadian goose, and deer, before the place became a Lyme disease factory, a haven for deer ticks and orange-clad hunters.

The spirit of the family survived in the kids who had carved their names into tree trunks. It survived in the root cellar, a pit of tree shoots, rotting branches, leaves, beer cans, and plastic. In the chimney that still stood against the wind. A hearth where an iron kettle once boiled vegetables, rabbit, and herbs, or laundry. The wide stone slab at the base of the fireplace had kept the dog warm and dried wet boots.

The impulse to tease Charlie had come over me once as I looked into his stupid face in the sixth grade, but something inside said, "Don't." My lips clamped shut.

I wanted to jab him—make him feel his dumbness, but something told me that he was too big and suffering.

When I heard what Charlie had done at the Amish school, the basic facts of his life seemed as shocking as his crime: That Charlie had married, had children, and drove a truck now seemed incongruous.

According to the news report, Charlie passed the school house daily on his route. His mind was twisted as the trees rent by yellow machines. He had given in to the impulse of boys spearing frogs. To me, he was still a boy crying in camo pants with the wet spot growing at his crotch—hands nailed to the sky.

Mathias and I found a toad by the base of the homestead chimney. He was brown with orange flecks behind his black bead eyes. His squared skull froze, his skin patterned with black paisley. A slice of silver crowned his eye. This was a good place for a frog or toad to live, where ferns sprouted.

The forest, where I find meaning, has claimed the Wentzel house and the trees buckled and torn. The silver-lidded toad waits to see what we will do. In his eye simmers the wild grapevine that consumes the stone.

They made a movie about the Amish shooting. I saw it on TV in a hotel lobby in Virginia. I mentioned to the clerk that I knew the guy who was the shooter. She didn't seem to care. My words were background noise, like cars and the cicada.

I wanted to go to Nickel Mines, now with Mathias. To look on the trees planted along the road where the girls had been killed, the school razed. To offer what I was writing or what I knew of Charlie. To question an Amish neighbor. To impose meaning on tragedy.

Instead, we stopped at a farmstand, and I told the girl in bare feet and a flower print dress to re-do her math and check the change. She smiled and told me that she still needed another quarter. Shy and simple words spoken with a Dutch lilt that flowers in my own speech at times.

I talked with Leon at the hardware store, and he told me to feed my giant pumpkins milk to grow them big. He invited me to his farm for horse manure and straw to build up my garden bed. The young clerks at the counter—one a boy with highlighted hair (English) and the other a teenage girl wearing a dress, her hair in a bun (Plain)—smiled at our talk about manure and peas, about spading flowerbeds. And Mathias listened.

Leon, like the roly poly, knows the dirt and shared his lore. He told me to turn the soil in rows during autumn and then to spread the straw and manure before the first frost. Loam the corn and pumpkin will want.

I didn't tell him my gardens were a wild tangle of purple cone flower and pumpkin, zucchini and sunflower fighting for space. I told him that last year, when the garden went wild while we were on vacation, one weed grew up in the asparagus patch that attracted all the Japanese beetles. I told him that instead of attacking my zucchini and vines, the metallic, clumped frenzy covered and devoured the leaves and stem of the weed.

Leon said that if the weed comes back again, save some seeds and spread it next year, to let weeds grow with the whispery asparagus.

Kirby Olson

HEADLIGHTS

"An East Stroudsburg girl and an Orlando, Fla. Man were killed
and three of their relatives seriously injured Monday, when the
sport utility vehicle the man was driving crashed as he took the
family back north from a Florida vacation."

—*Pocono Record*

The 3-dollar bill
is baloney.

The ankle
is macaroni.

Waterfalls fall,
clouds cloud,
rivers arrive.

The road curves,
cars collide.

Kirby Olson

NOCTURNAL CAFÉ BY VAN GOGH

Amid a disarray of chairs and cups, a turquoise
waitress commands order; stars explode within the struggle.
A funereal horse & buggy carry the news of an exotic party.
A lonely observer, Van Gogh is invited to view the convivial.

I piece together his ghoulish skies.
In a crooked window, a cat licks her paws with a raspy tongue.

The vast expanse of turquoise cobblestones
evanesce beneath a chromatic yellow awning.
Various reds. The gaslight comes at a slant.
Heavily coated men walk against it, and the
broken roofs of the poor lean together.

Bray McDonald

METAMORPHOSIS

If in the end each man finds the answer
none will find it what they thought it to be.

What child before it leaves its mother's womb
can comprehend what its name shall be?

Can a caterpillar precisely predict
the many colors of the butterfly?

Bray McDonald

FAITH

Tree leaves congregate
To worship a holy sun
They can only feel

Frank Cavano

PIECES OF DREAMS

And as for fishing in streams, for pieces of dreams, those pieces will never fit. What is the sense of it?

—Michel Legrand

I MET HIM ON THE EAST BRANCH of the Ausable River on a Saturday afternoon, my planned escape from the constant demands of graduate school. Rounding a corner of the serpentine stream, I surprised him, as he drew a cigarette from his vest and prepared to take a break from his pursuit of large brown trout.

Jesse, looking up through horned rimmed glasses, nodded and smiled warmly at me, a potential interloper.

"Any luck?" I offered, following the fisherman's code of respectful inquiry.

Jesse opened his creel and revealed three beautiful browns replete with orange rings and bellies the color of creamery butter.

I returned the favor, gaining a smile of admiration from the diminutive angler.

For the next two hours, Jesse shared his boulder on the Ausable and some of his perspectives on life.

I would never be quite the same, nor would it become clear to me why I had begun to pour forth my frustrations to this fellow angler.

Jesse listened, nodded his head and smiled. When he did comment, his responses seemed strange and not to the point.

Nevertheless, I continued to vent, barely taking a breath between installments. First, I told him of the enormous work load at school to which he replied, "That's quite a dream."

Undaunted, I filled in all the details including the overdue term paper and the approach of final exams.

Jesse placed a friendly hand on my shoulder but said no more.

I told him that Jane had wanted us to marry, but I could not fit marriage into my plans for a successful career. So, I ended the relationship and now felt both sad and guilty about that decision.

Jesse smiled and stated, "One is always doing the best he can at any given time."

Less than satisfied with this response, I pushed onward. I told him next about the problems with my family of origin, how I found myself in great conflict whenever a member of the clan insisted that I take his or her side in a family battle.

"They but dream separate dreams," Jesse said and smiled. "You need not judge which dream is best."

By this time, it was becoming clear that, each time Jesse spoke, nodded, or smiled, brief periods of peacefulness were given me. No, they did not last, but they were lovely nevertheless.

But I had not hit him with the biggest problems yet. Dare I disclose such things to this stranger?

Before I could consider the pros and cons of such disclosure I found myself "spilling the beans," and all of them. There were the things I had done, and the things I had failed to do. There were my sinful acts, my sinful words, my sinful thoughts, and even the many times I had placed myself in situation which might have been "near occasions of sin." I covered grade school, girls, and adolescence. I spoke of my cutthroat competition for grades and competition on the ball field. I revealed the time I had injured my friend in a fight and the anger I had felt, at one time or another, toward every member of the family. Words and feelings poured from me like river water in a spring flood.

The push of guilt was so strong that, for a time, I dared not make eye contact with Jesse.

At last, I searched his face for a reaction and found only the warmest of smiles. The scolding I had anticipated never came. Peace was visiting me once more, and this time, it lingered.

How surprised I was that, in the midst of such serenity, I soon found myself blurting out, "But what about hell, Jesse"?

Jesse withdrew two cigarettes from his fishing vest and handed one of them to me. "There is no hell to pursue us beyond the grave, my brother. Hell is merely what our thoughts would make of this life." With that, he uttered, "Thanks for the talk," and headed downstream.

I watched until he disappeared into the sunshine.

I would never see Jesse again in the flesh, but his kind mind and loving heart remained with me as I faced the ups and downs of circumstance, meeting life on its terms day in and day out.

Eventually, I came to see life as a puzzle which could not and need not be solved. Perfection was no longer a goal for me, and I seemed to be easier on others, as well as myself. I settled for good moments in the present and focused less on the past and the future.

In a conflict-ridden situation, I was capable, at times, of assuming a position of not knowing, rather than forming a judgment and insisting that my position was the correct one.

Finally, and perhaps most importantly, a great change came about in the way I perceived God. I now viewed our Source as always-forgiving and totally-loving.

These changes had, it seemed, succeeded in removing guilt's ghostly garland from my shoulders. This was no small gift.

ABOUT TEN YEARS AFTER THE AFTERNOON with Jesse on the Ausable, I found myself fishing a small stream for brook trout, more than a hundred miles from my home. As noon approached, I retired to a nearby diner for lunch. Perusing the local rag, I came upon the death notices and obituary section, where I encountered a photo of Jesse Charles Reuter. His earthly life had come to an end in a tragic automobile accident.

Choking back tears, I found myself reflecting on our meeting and how this small but ever-so-powerful man had changed my perspectives on life. He had done so with smiles, a few well-chosen words, and an absolute refusal to accept my self-accusations and guilt.

I uttered a prayer of thanks.

Driving homeward, I considered returning to the area in a week or two to locate and visit Jesse's grave, but I did not do that.

Somehow, I knew he was not there.

Guy R. Beining

PLANETARY BEING

Being in the green
smoke, being of
rock & tree,
a figure not
meant to be
more than a blind
spot in the
universal pull—
always in that
passage between tide
& pulse, a sand
bar of another era,
something unbrushed,
unknown.

Steve Jordan

LEANING

I'll wait for the song
more sacred than you,
one worn thumb befriending steel strings.
Loose strums and cracked words want
no home in a microphone, will meet
no walls and no ceiling,
and instead will slip away off the dusty porch
into the dusk,
barely moving past the fence
as the wind sinks them into the grass.
Ramshackle warble,
a yellowthroat flying in aimless circles,
a one-speed bike coasting
with feet off the pedals.
Your face twists
as you play a song to the train tracks
to a slow rattler,
its door sliding shut,
rolling everywhere that's in between.
I'll head back to Tanzania,
buy a cheap Fanta and lean
in a doorway
on a sunny Tuesday afternoon;
the place where I finally stopped
and saw that all roads looped back
to where I was.

Florica Elena Lorint

THE LOGGER KING

ONCE UPON A TIME in a faraway country there was a king called Mugur who wanted to marry the most intelligent young woman in his kingdom. With this in mind, King Mugur sent messengers everywhere. They traveled across the country and back, from the North to the South, and from the East to the West.

A great number of young women arrived at the royal court. All were welcome. Some were tall, some short, some were plain, and some beautiful; but, they were all very intelligent. They had been summoned by the messengers and arrived at the court, each more desirable than the one before.

A great feast was prepared in their honor, and King Mugur's court gathered and participated in the meal and ceremony.

The Master of Ceremonies showed great inspiration. Large tables groaned with endless platters of food from every corner of the land, imaginatively carved or molded into all sorts of flowers and animals. The feast was served on silver chargers and in crystal bowls, surrounded by candles of purest white, on pale blue cloths woven for the occasion.

Everyone was amazed by such elegance. The beautiful food and wine, the musicians and dancers who entertained, all bordered upon perfection.

Only King Mugur did not seem satisfied. He barely touched the delectable morsels and the exquisite wine. He was waiting for something more.

All of a sudden, the guards opened the palace gates, and the procession of young women made its appearance.

The King rose and slowly climbed to the massive and elegant throne, his rightful place. The Marshal of the Guards brought the scepter to the King, and the King nodded. The introduction of the women could begin.

The women began to parade before the King, gracious even as they were awed by the opulence and grandeur.

King Mugur demanded that each young woman kneel before him to answer the three questions he would pose. The reply needed to be spontaneous, amusing, and full of good sense, all at once.

One after another the young women passed in front of the King and tried their best to respond as he wished to the three questions, but no reply pleased the King.

His messengers' long search and the subsequent royal feast seemed doomed to failure.

King Mugur's entourage tried to find other solutions, but all attempts were in vain. The King would not pose another question as they suggested, nor would he choose the most beautiful.

Finally, the King decided to leave the palace and search for the young bride of whom he had always dreamed—the most intelligent young girl of his kingdom, one he would consider dignified enough to share the responsibilities of his life.

So said, so done.

Disguised as a logger, young King Mugur left his palace in the city and headed out alone into his kingdom. He allowed no one to accompany him, for the trip was to remain a secret. Even his mother did not know of the journey. She would have worried and begged him to stay, or at least to take men to protect him.

Full of courage, King Mugur took to the road, alone for the first time in his life.

King Mugur traveled throughout his country for many months without succeeding in finding the young woman of his dreams; however, he remained convinced that his efforts would be rewarded.

One beautiful summer evening, he arrived in a small village to which he had felt inexplicably attracted. Enchanted, King Mugur chose, seemingly by chance, a small house and knocked on the door.

A young, beautiful woman named Calina opened the door. "Welcome, stranger. Please come in. You must be tired."

The King did not wait for a second invitation. He walked straight into the kitchen and dropped his bag behind the door.

Turning slowly, King Mugur looked around the kitchen and turned to her. "You are receiving me into your house, young woman, without even knowing who I am. If the King of this country opened the frontiers to all strangers, the enemies would take over and destroy our homes. Don't you believe so?"

Calina kept her smile. "The laws of the kingdom are not the same as those of the house, Sire. It's up to you to decide what's good for the country and up to me to decide what's good for my home."

Mugur the King was astonished to be so quickly recognized. "How do you know who I am?"

"It's very simple, Sire. I can see in your face the shadow of the worries that the kingdom bestows on you. Meanwhile, upon your head, I can see the traces of the heavy crown you usually wear."

The King liked her reply. He looked at her more closely and considered her with more attention. "You are a young, beautiful woman with a rich abundance of lovely hair. Can you tell me how many hairs you have?"

"Seven-million, Sire."

"How can you tell with such precision? Have you counted them?"

"If you don't believe me, you are welcome to count them yourself."

The King began to laugh. Again, he admitted that the young girl showed intelligence, and now she showed even a sense of humor.

"Alright, tomorrow morning I will go into the forest and cut wood. If, upon my return, you will receive me with the biggest surprise of my life, you will become the Queen of this country."

The next morning, King Mugur left for the forest. Carrying his bag of heavy tools, he walked deep into the forest before he began to cut wood. He worked all day chopping wood and did not return before nightfall. He was deeply tired, for he was not accustomed to such hard work.

He returned to Calina's home and dragged his tools through the door. He stopped in the middle of the room. "Well, Calina, where is my surprise?"

The young woman was arranging the dinner table and its humble fare. She answered in a gentle voice, "The house is in order, Sire. The same is true for the yard and the garden. Dinner is ready, and it is delicious. I was waiting for you impatiently, not because you are the King, but because I want you for yourself. That is the surprise I have for you."

Florica Elena Lorint

THE NIGHT OF SAINT JOHN

ONCE UPON A TIME, there was a farmer. Doru had his house, his fields, and his animals. In short, he had everything he needed; he was healthy and full of strength with a fine family. However, he had never been fully contented with his life. Why?

All of his friends, his wife, and his children were asking the same question: Why?

One day while our man was working in the barnyard of the farm with his usual long face, he saw a stranger walking along the road. The farmer did not stop working. At least, he did not intend to stop.

The stranger approached the fence and greeted the farmer. "I have traveled a great distance. I am a cattle merchant, and I am headed to the market not too far away. Two of my animals are very tired. I can't make them go any farther. If you will keep them here for a short time, I will pay you very well," he said.

"How long shall I keep them, and what kind of animals do you have?" Doru asked. He wanted to make sure he knew what was in store for him. After all, these could be troublesome beasts.

"Oh, let's say a few weeks, maybe until the end of June. I have two donkeys named Immediately and Wait A Minute."

The farmer found the donkeys' names strange, but he did not wish to offend the stranger. After all, had he not chosen their names?

Keeping the donkeys for a few weeks—Why not?

The fields were blooming, and the two animals could graze wherever they pleased. The stranger was even going to pay for this service. After all, Doru had so many animals on the farm that he figured two more would not be noticed.

"It's a deal. You can trust me, Stranger. I will keep your beasts. Immediately and Wait A Minute will be well taken care of and nourished by my vast fields," he said.

The two feeble donkeys were led to the farmer. Without a doubt, the animals had known better days. Quietly, as though they understood the deal between the two men, they entered the barn and lay down in the clean hay.

"They are very intelligent, your donkeys. I am astonished."

"Oh, yes," agreed the stranger with a mysterious smile forming on his lips. "You see, we humans believe that the animals are far less intelligent than we, while in reality..."

"In reality, what?" Doru was curious now.

"In reality, the beasts are often much more intelligent than people. They have extraordinary powers and gifts, like these two donkeys whom you have received with hospitality usually extended only to people."

"Gifts? What kind of gifts?" interrupted the farmer. His greedy eyes grew large as he whirled around to face the stranger.

"Well, like many other animals, these two donkeys talk to each other during the Night of Saint John."

Doru was disappointed. "I know that the animals speak among themselves all the time, but we cannot understand what they are saying."

The merchant let the farmer finish what he had to say before speaking. "During the Night of Saint John, the animals talk and even inanimate objects speak. The one who knows how to listen closely with respect and patience can discover the secrets of life."

After the merchant spoke in this manner, he waved goodbye, and with a last look at his beasts, he left the barnyard.

Doru decided to keep their conversation to himself, thinking that all he had heard was more likely legend than truth. Learning mysteries from animals and objects, discovering the secrets of life, these gifts did not seem possible. He scratched his head, shrugged his shoulders, and returned to his daily work.

Doru had almost forgotten his strange encounter with the merchant, when all of a sudden an unusual but friendly noise came from the stable. The farmer hurried to his barn, for he knew too well he needed to feed and water the two animals that were now resting.

"Wait a minute," yelled the farmer, trying to reassure the two beasts. But, the one who had this name started braying loudly.

"Immediately," the farmer yelled again, not knowing where to turn.

Cacophony filled the barn as the other animals joined in with their own voices. The sound grew louder, a veritable concert of instruments tuning up.

At first, the farmer felt his blood boiling, but after awhile he started to laugh. He realized what he had said. At the bottom of his heart, he was a man who was kind and generous and truly cared for animals. Time went by as it always does, day after day, night after night, then weeks and months.

FOR THE SAINT JOHN'S HOLIDAY, the villagers near Doru's farm made provisions of wood, wine, and food. The farmer did the same. Only late at night did he remember the words of the strange merchant who was supposed to return soon for his two donkeys.

What a pity that he would return. By now, Doru had grown fond of the two animals, sometimes gentle, sometimes stubborn. The two donkeys were treated like kings by the other animals, for due to their condition, the farmer spared them from the hard labor of the farm.

Now, the farmer remembered the merchant's words and thought, "Today is Saint John's Night. The beasts will talk."

Without delay, he hurried to the stables. The two donkeys were finishing the hay they had received for dinner. Wait A Minute was eating slowly, as if he had all the time in the world to enjoy his share. Immediately was chomping and gulping his food as if it were to be his last meal.

As midnight arrived, the two donkeys suddenly began speaking to each other. Doru was astonished to find that indeed he could understand every word of their conversation.

"If our host knew," commented Immediately, "that at the roots of the large walnut tree in his garden there is buried a large treasure, he would become the richest man in the world."

"Yes, yes, if our host knew...that the buried treasure at the roots of the walnut tree...in the middle of his garden..." Wait A Minute always drawled and hesitated.

Doru did not wait to hear the end of Wait A Minute's reply. He was already on his way to dig up the hidden treasure buried at the roots of the walnut tree. There, he found seven large bags full of gold and precious stones.

"Aha." He danced and sang joyous songs. "I have all the reasons to be content and happy. My worries are over. I am the richest man in the world."

This was true. He had become the richest man in the world.

Soon, he was spending day and night counting his new wealth and worrying over the treasure. He had no more time for his animals and farm, or for his family, friends, and neighbors. His children married and left the house. His wife grew old. His friends never invited him to their homes, anymore. He had turned them down so many times now that they had grown tired of his refusals. And so, despite all his riches, the farmer felt sad and lonely.

IT WAS AGAIN MANY YEARS LATER the Eve of Saint John's Night. The farmer remembered the two donkeys that he had not seen for so long. Counting his wealth took so much time that he had hired others to care of his animals and farm. Were the donkeys still alive? The best way to find out was to go see for himself. One never knew what might happen on the Night of Saint John.

Oh yes, the two donkeys were there and, just at the stroke of midnight, Wait A Minute and Immediately began to speak again. Surprisingly, the animal Wait A Minute, slow by nature, was finishing the phrase he had started so long ago, "If our host knew…that the buried treasure…at the roots of the…walnut tree in the middle… of his garden…would only bring loneliness and unhappiness to his life…, he would never dig it up. He would be far happier living as a simple farmer, much happier."

The farmer understood the lesson. He solemnly said, "Thank you."

From that day on, the farmer returned to living as he always had, tending his own animals, spending time with his family and friends. With his money, he helped the poor.

Thereafter, he became a contented and happy man. Often, the people in the village and his friends came to him for advice.

He always advised, "Wait a minute; let me think first."

One day, while he was bringing water and food to the two donkeys, he noticed a stranger in the courtyard. Upon looking closer, this man seemed familiar to him. Here, after all these years, was the merchant who had come back for his two donkeys. Doru felt a tug at his heart.

After greeting the farmer, the merchant asked to see his donkeys.

Having lived by the wise words of "Wait A Minute" for some years, Doru, the farmer saw that this was now the right place and time to call on the other donkey. So, he said, "Immediately."

Cory Russo

THE JASMINE REVOLUTION

I ONCE READ THAT THE JASMINE FLOWER is the flower of revolution—sweet but strong, and representing unity. In fact, notable fights for equality and freedom in various parts of the world have been referred to as the Jasmine Revolution. It's no surprise that her name is Jasmine. Her. My sister.

The first time I was able to proclaim aloud that I had a biological sister was a few days before my 33rd birthday. I had found her. My heart pounded and fluttered like a caged bird inside of my chest, as if I were close to freedom. But how would I message her and tell her how I always felt I had siblings and that now I knew? How would I tell her she had a sister after we had both lived our lives not knowing for sure that the other existed?

I clicked on her page, ready to send the message. Then, at the top of the page I saw the word, "Remembering."

Remembering what? It couldn't be that people were merely remembering her immeasurable existence at the age of 29—could it? That she was not present? That she had died three weeks before I found her? It couldn't be that kind of remembering.

At that moment, I discovered I could grieve someone I had never met, someone who had shared the same womb that had nurtured me just a few years later.

Maybe that's why I didn't need to meet her to feel that she was my sister. I could already see my smile in hers, the energy behind our eyes operating at the same frequency, the empathy in our hearts, the flow of our pens composing similar poetry, our fists most likely raised together at peace rallies at least once, and the same ink tatooed onto our skin to express ourselves, because there's not enough art in the world to paint the compassion deep within our souls.

Both of us had been placed with families that fostered our growth and loved us so hard that we had no choice but to love the world back, to be ourselves. So had our brother, he who feels like the strong roots to our branches,

When I visited the house where she grew up and met her family, I felt instantly at home because I felt her. Her mother and father cried when they heard my laugh, because despite our being raised apart, the genetics couldn't be denied. I could almost visualize our DNA strands intertwining as I walked through the door, as if science had made an exception for us.

I sank onto her parents' carpet, and they noted that she also loved sitting on the floor. I don't think chairs were made for us. We liked to be grounded. Maybe, gravity gave us the courage that society so often tried to strip from us. Maybe, we fell to our knees after long days because fighting for equality becomes exhausting.

I witnessed the stages of her growth through pictures and videos. Each snapshot imprinted itself into my memory, while I sat wishing she would walk into the room and hug me for the first time.

I visited her grave at the Jewish cemetery. There, stones are placed rather than flowers because stones never die. Besides, she already represents to me one of the strongest flowers.

That day, I fell to my knees at her grave to try to be as close I as I could to her. That day, I wore a shirt that read "Nevertheless, she persisted." As it turned out, this shirt was the same one she had worn the day she died.

The rabbi said no relationship in our lives lasts as long as that of a sibling. Our relationship hadn't even begun.

Now, her laughter consumes my dreams, but I wake up to a daily nightmare—the reality that the longing for the bond of two sisters may never pass. The rabbi also said that, at some level of existence we cannot understand, this too was intended.

She understands what we cannot now, because the most beautiful flowers are picked first, by children running through gardens. Their subconscious knows that life will be cut short, yet their hands can't be restrained, pulling the natural beauty of flowers from the earth to make someone else smile in the way she did. *Dayenu*. Hebrew for "it would've been enough."

It would've been enough for me to meet her just once. For even one minute of earth time. One minute in physical form. To tell her that when she left us, she would never have to sit on confining chairs again. She would never have to worry about her name being spoken for the last time, never have to worry about her husband loving anything more than he loves her, never have to worry about her students, because they will learn more from this than they ever have, never have to worry about poetry being unwritten in the molecules that would leave an everlasting impression on the universe, never have to worry about someone halting her fight for humanity, because I will fight even harder now.

It would've been enough to tell her she was strong and that cancer would never kill her spirit. That nevertheless, she persisted, like a stone that is permanent, never dies. Like her. Her. My sister.

CONTRIBUTOR NOTES

JODY AZZOUNI was born in Brooklyn, New York and started writing at the age of 12. His fantasies and dreams involve nothing visual—just a lot of words, often in dialogue. (Imagine a great darkness with subtitles.) He also teaches philosophy at Tufts and lives in a library.

GUY BEINING is the author of *The Silence of My Room* (Chintamani Books, 2018), as well as more than fifty collections and chapbooks of poetry. He was awarded the PIP Gertrude Stein Award for Innovative Poetry in English 2005-2006. His artwork has been featured on the covers of literary magazines and exhibited throughout the United States, from the Hudson Opera House to Louisiana Tech University.

JOSEPH BOTTONE was born in Brooklyn, New York and educated in the city streets and the wild woods of the Catskill Mountains. He studied horticulture and practiced the art of wise-water-use-landscape-design. Later, he was poet-in-residence for some years at Camaldoli Monastery in Big Sur, California. He has published in the *Paris Review*, the *Malpais Review*, *Abraxas*, *Oriental Blue Streak*, *Avocet*, the *World*, *Fixed and Free* anthology, and others.

CLIFFORD BROWDER is a writer living in New York City. He is the author of two biographies, a novel, and an award-winning selection of posts from his blog "No Place for Normal: New York." His poetry has appeared in *Runes*, *Heliotrope*, *Snake Nation Review*, the *Brillantina Project*, the *Forever Journal*, *GNU Journal*, and elsewhere.

RICHARD ALAN BUNCH is a three-time Pushcart Prize nominee and the author of several collections of poetry, including *Moonlit Plazas and Wild Swans* (Infinity Publishing, 2014); *Collected Poems: 1965-2011* (Infinity Publishing, 2012); and *Running for Daybreak* (Edwin Mellen Press, 2004). His poetry has appeared in the *Windsor Review*, *Poetry New Zealand*, the *Hurricane Review*, *Poem*, the *Hawai'i Review*, *Many Mountains Moving*, the *Xavier Review*, *Slant*, the *Homestead Review*, *Dirigible*, *Haight Ashbury Literary Journal*, the *West Wind Review*, the *Comstock Review*, and the *Oregon Review*. He resides with his family in Davis, California.

EDWARD BRUCE BYNUM, Ph.D., A.B.P.P., is a clinical psychologist and the Director of Behavioral Medicine at the University of Massachusetts Health Services in Amherst. A student of Chandrasekharananad Saraswati and a winner of the Abraham H. Maslow award from the American Psychological Association, he is the author of four books, including *Dark Light Consciousness* (Inner Traditions, 2012).

FRANK CAVANO is a retired physician whose writings attempt to comment on the complexity of the human condition with all its fragility, pain, *pathos*, and beauty. Many of his efforts invoke a spiritual or inspirational perspective. In the last ten years, more than 120 of his pieces have found a home online and/or in print. He is always grateful when a poem stimulates new thought or strikes an emotional chord with a reader.

NOEL CONNEELY has published poems in *Chelsea*, *Main Street Rag*, the *Coe Review*, the *Yellow Medicine Review*, the *Willow Review*, and other publications throughout Ireland and the United States. He has taught Irish for many years in Dunlavin.

JAMIE DONOHOE, whose roller derby sobriquet is Mr. Sparkles, is a teacher, actor, father, and husband who writes drama and poetry, instead of folding laundry. "It's a political thing," he often tells his wife. His writing has most recently appeared in the *Cape Rock*, *Freefall* and the *William and Mary Review*.

EVE VAN DYKE is a filmmaker and writer based in Brooklyn, New York. She is a Fulbright scholar.

CRAIG EVENSON is a school teacher. He shares a house with some dogs, cats, parrots, and a woman.

CHERYL J. FISH's fiction has been featured in *Liars League NYC* and (a short story from the innovative lit mag *Between C&D*) in an exhibit at the Fales Library, New York University. An excerpt from her novel manuscript *Off the Yoga Mat* was a finalist in L Magazine's Literary Upstart contest. Her most recent poetry chapbook is *Make It Funny, Make it Last* (#171, Belladonna, 2014). Her work has appeared in the *Bloomsbury Anthology of Contemporary Jewish American Poetry* (Bloomsbury Academic, 2013), *Terrain.org*, *New American Writing*, *Talisman*, the *Village Voice*, the *Santa Monica Review*, *Hanging Loose*, the *Kudzu House Review*, *Reed Magazine*, *Volt*, and the *Gyroscope Review*. Her prose on travel literature and environmental justice in film and literature has appeared in various journals and books. She has been Fulbright professor in Finland, writer-in-residence at Mount St. Helens National Volcanic Monument, and she is professor of English at Borough of Manhattan Community College, City University of New York.

HALEY GUARIGLIA grew up in the creeks of Columbia, Missouri and currently resides in Kansas City, Missouri with her boyfriend and 18-year-old cat, Fedora. Her interests include interpretive dance, bugs, costume creation, and reading aloud. Her favorite poet of 2016 is Kate Marvin. Worth mentioning is her love for Philip Schultz and Gabrielle Calvecoressi. She can be found online on her blog at http://www.itwillbeallwrite-itwillbeallright.com/

GREGORY GILBERT GUMBS was born on the small Dutch island of Aruba, in the Caribbean. He has worked as a criminologist, lawyer, and screenwriter, and has published poems in anthologies and magazines in many countries, including the Netherlands, England, France, Ireland, Australia, and India. His screenplay *Melting Ice* won screenwriting awards in the United States and Europe. He is finishing up his first book of poems, creative nonfiction, essays, drawings, and artwork entitled *I'll Never Forget*.

A ten-time Pushcart Prize nominee, GEORGE HELD publishes widely both online and in print. His recent poetry chapbooks are *Phased II* (Poets Wear Prada, 2016) and *Dog Hill Poems* (Goldfish Press, 2017). A retired professor of English at Queens College (CUNY), George lives in Greenwich Village with his wife, Cheryl.

ROBERT HIRSCHFIELD is a New York-based poet and prose writer whose work appears in *Salamander*, *Tablet*, the *Jewish Review of Books*, *Sojourners*, and many other publications. The poem "Kathmandu Morning" was inspired by Nepal's wild convergence of the spiritual and natural realms, along with the commercial and electronic realms.

MATTHEW T. HUMMER is a teacher and writer from Pennsylvania. His writing has been published in journals such as *Stone Voices*, *Zymbol*, *Stoneboat*, and *Agave Magazine*. Links to his other writing and art can be found at: http://scribenswriting.weebly.com/.

STEVE JORDAN grew up in the Chicagoland area. He earned an M.F.A. in Creative Writing from Northwestern University and an Ed.M. from Harvard Graduate School of Education. He studied poetry at Harvard University with Joanna Klink. His work has appeared in *Lyrical Somerville* and *Third Wednesday*. Steve teaches high school English in Cambridge, Massachusetts.

REBECCA LILLY is the author of several books of *haiku*, some in collaboration with visual artists: *Shadwell Hills* (Birch Brook Press, 2002), *Yesterday's Footprints* (Red Moon Press, 2012), *A Prism of Wings* (Antrim House, 2013), and *Light's Reservoir* (Antrim House, 2013). *Light's Reservoir*, a book of *haiku* on wildflowers, was a *Foreword Reviews* finalist in the nature category for 2013. Lilly holds an M.F.A. in Creative Writing from Cornell University and a Ph.D. in Philosophy from Princeton University.

BRAY MCDONALD is a graduate of the University of South Alabama and studied poetry under Sue Brannan Walker and Walt Darring. Mr. McDonald has been published in many journals recently, including the *Black Scat Review*, *Big Muddy*, the *Blue Collar Review*, the *Cape Rock*, the *Clackamas Literary Review*, *Opiate*, *Quiddity*, and *Third Wednesday*. He also has poetry forthcoming in *Storyteller Magazine* and *Gold Dust*.

FLORICA ELENA LORINT was a Canadian-Romanian author of specialty literature. She passed away leaving a manuscript of unpublished fairy tales. The stories in this issue are excerpted from that manuscript.

TARA MENON is a freelance writer based in Lexington, Massachusetts. Her poems have appeared in *Calliope*, *Azizah Magazine*, *Aaduna*, *10x3 plus*, and an anthology, *Yellow as Turmeric, Fragrant as Cloves* (Deep Bowl Press, 2008). Her stories and reviews have also appeared in journals including the *Green Mountains Review*, *Fjords Literary Review*, *Calyx*, *Many Mountains Moving*, the *South Carolina Review*, and *India Currents*.

GREG MOGLIA is a veteran of 27 years as Adjunct Professor of Philosophy of Education at New York University and 37 years as a high school teacher of physics and psychology. His poems have been accepted in over 300 journals in seven countries. He lives in Huntington, New York.

RICK MURPHY is the author of *The Apple in the Monkey Tree* (Codhill Press, 2007), *Voyeur* (Gival Press, 2009), and *Body Politic* (Prolific Press, 2017). He is also the author of several chapbooks. His recent poetry appears in the *Transnational*, *BlazeVox*, the *Pennsylvania Review*, *Literati Quarterly*, and others.

A veteran, former hospice nurse, and ex-roughneck (as on oil rigs), AYAZ DARYL NIELSEN has been editor of the print publication *bear creek haiku* for 25+ years and over 135 issues. Ayaz can be found online at https://bearcreekhaiku.blogspot.com. His poetry, published worldwide, includes *senryu* chosen in 2010 and 2012 as "Best of Year" by the Irish Haiku Association. He is also the author of a chapbook, Window Left Open (Prolific Press, 2017). Along with other deeply appreciated honors, he is especially delighted by the depth and quality of poets worldwide whose poems have found homes in *bear creek haiku*'s print and online presence.

KIRBY OLSON is a professor at SUNY Delhi in the western Catskills. He is the author of the poetry collection *Christmas at Rockefeller Center* (WordTech Editions, 2015).

JARED PEARCE teaches writing and literature at William Penn University. His poems have recently been or will soon be shared in *Glass Kite*, *Infinity's Kitchen*, *Gyroscope*, *DIAGRAM*, and *Fieldstone Review*.

SIMON PERCHIK is an attorney whose poems have appeared in the *Partisan Review*, *Forge*, *Poetry*, *Osiris*, the *New Yorker* and elsewhere. His most recent collection is *The Osiris Poems* (box of chalk, 2017). For more information, including free e-books and his essay titled "Magic, Illusion and Other Realities," please visit his website at www.simonperchik.com.

JENNIFER RAHA earned her M.F.A. in 2013 from UNC Greensboro, where she was a Fred Chappell Fellow. She was a finalist in Nazim Hikmet's 2013 Poetry Festival, as well as the Crab Orchard Review's 2013 Allison Joseph Poetry Prize. She teaches high school English in southeastern Virginia. Her writings have recently appeared in *Triquarterly*, the *Santa Clara Review*, the *Cresset*, and *Blue Lyra*.

MARILYN RINGER has been a chef and restauranteur, a poet-teacher with California's Poets-in-the-Schools, and a teacher of adult creative writing workshops. Her work has appeared in *Red Wheelbarrow*, the *Griffin*, *Watershed*, *California Quarterly*, *Milk Money*, *Pearl*, and others. During the summer, she writes on Monhegan Island in Maine with a group of women who are artists, teachers, Gestalt therapists, and gardeners, as well as writers.

TIM ROBBINS teaches ESL and does freelance translation from French. He has been a regular contributor to *Hanging Loose* since 1978. He is the author of a poetry collection entitled *Denny's Arbor Vitae* (Adelaide Books, 2017).

CORY RUSSO is a writer and spoken word artist who first found her stage in Las Vegas, all while completing undergraduate and graduate school. She reveals herself slowly through her words recorded on albums, a published children's book, and readings in venues across the country.

DANIEL PATRICK SCOTT is the author of two short-story collections, *Some of Us Have to Get Up in the Morning* (Turtle Point Pres, 2001) and *Pay This Amount* (Laughing Fire Press, 2008), as well as a novel, *Valedictory* (Savant Books, 2015). He is the recipient of various awards from the Christopher Isherwood Foundation, the New York Foundation for the Arts, and the MacDowell Colony. His work has appeared in many magazines and anthologies, most recently *Best Gay Stories* 2016. He lives in New York City.

J. T. TOWNLEY has published in the *Harvard Review, Hayden's Ferry Review, Prairie Schooner,* the *Threepenny Review,* and other magazines and journals. His stories have been nominated for the Pushcart Prize and Best of the Net award. He holds an M.F.A. in Creative Writing from the University of British Columbia and an M.Phil. in English from Oxford University. He teaches at the University of Virginia. To learn more, visit jttownley.com.

JOHN J. TRAUSE, the Director of Oradell Public Library, is the author of *Picture This: For Your Eyes and Ears* (Dos Madres Press, 2016), *Exercises in High Treason* (great weather for MEDIA, 2016), *Eye Candy for Andy: 13 Most Beautiful… Poems for Andy Warhol's Screen Tests* (Finishing Line Press, 2013), *Inside Out, Upside Down, and Round and Round* (Nirala Publications, 2012), *Seriously Serial* (Poets Wear Prada, 2007; rev. ed. 2014), and *Latter-Day Litany* (Éditions élastiques, 1996), the latter staged Off Broadway. He has also written a book of traditional and experimental poems, *Why Sing?* (Sensitive Skin Press, 2017). His translations, poetry, and visual work appear internationally in many journals and anthologies, including the *Antioch Review, Crossings, Maintenant, Offerta Speciale*, the Great Weather for Media anthologies *It's Animal but Merciful* (2012) and *I Let Go of the Stars in My Hand* (2014), and *Rabbit Ears: TV Poems* (NYQ Books, 2015). Marymark Press has published his visual poetry and art as broadsides and sheets. He is the subject of a 30/30/30 series essay written by Don Zirilli and published on the Operating System (operatingsytem.org). He is also the author of an essay on Baroness Elsa at the same site. Finally, he is a founder of the William Carlos Williams Poetry Cooperative in Rutherford, New Jersey, and the former host and curator of its monthly reading series.

KIMBERLY WHITE's poetry has appeared in the *Massachusetts Review, Cream City Review, Big Muddy, Dark Matter*, and other journals and anthologies. She is the author of two novels: *Bandy's Restola* (Purple Couchworks, 2011) and *Hotel Tarantula* (Lulu, 2014). Find poetry and collage art on her website, www.purplecouchworks.com, as well as on Facebook and various refrigerator doors.

Pediatrician KELLEY JEAN WHITE has worked in inner city Philadelphia and rural New Hampshire. Her poems have appeared in *Exquisite Corpse*, *Rattle*, and *JAMA*. Her recent books are *Toxic Environment* (Boston Poet Press, 2008) and *Two Birds in Flame* (Beech River Books, 2010). She received a 2008 Pennsylvania Council on the Arts grant.

KRISTIN CAMITTA ZIMET is the author of *Take in My Arms the Dark* (1999) and the Editor of the *Sow's Ear Poetry Review*. Her poems are in a great many journals in the United States and abroad, among them *Lilith*, *Salt Hill*, *Crab Orchard Review*, and *Poet Lore*. Her newest manuscript explores voices from Torah.

SUBSCRIBE

P.O. Box 131, Planetarium Station;
New York, NY 10024

_____$12 One-Year Subscribtion (one annual issue)

_____$20 Two-Year Subscription (two annual issues)

Please include $4.95 for postage and handling and enclose a check written to *Lalitamba*.

Begin my subscription with issue number _____

Name_____

Address_____

City, State, Zip_____

Please send a gift subscription to:

Begin the subscription with issue number _____

Name_____

Address_____

City, State, Zip_____

LALITAMBA SARANAM

P.O. Box 131, Planetarium Station; New York, NY 10024

Lalitamba partners with Lalitamba Saranam, a holistic homeless shelter in New York City. Through years of working with people in need of permanent housing, we understand how stressful the situation can be. Lalitamba Saranam offers the comforts of home to women in transition, including survivors of domestic violence and runaway youth.

• Social Services

• Life Skills

• Art Studio

• Yoga, Meditation, and Massage

• Clothing Boutique

• Street Outreach

• Soup Kitchen

To make a tax-deductible donation to the shelter, please mail a check to Lalitamba Saranam at the above address. Your generosity makes it all possible. Thank you!

www.threejewelsrefuge.org

CHINTAMANI BOOKS
www.chintamanibooks.org

Chintamani Books is a 501(c)3 non-profit press that was founded to offer book donations to hospital patients, prison inmates, and the homeless population.

We published our first volume at the request of a dedicated group of detox patients at the Addiction Institute, who had experienced our inpatient poetry-and-meditation workshops and wished to study further. Since then, we have grown to offer good reads in fiction, nonfiction, poetry, and translation. Chintamani Books is also the publisher of Lalitamba magazine.

To submit, please send a proposal letter and sample pages/full manuscript in hard copy to:

Lalitamba/Chintamani Books
P.O. Box 131
Planetarium Station
New York, NY 10024

Please include SASE for reply. If you would like your manuscript returned, please provide postage; otherwise, the manuscript will be recycled.

NOTE: Poetry manuscripts should include at least 65 poems/pages.

www.ingramcontent.com/pod-product-compliance
Lightning Source LLC
Chambersburg PA
CBHW020433180626
46812CB00003B/1206